The Constitution

of the

United States

The Constitution of the United States

*   *   *   *

With Case Summaries

Bicentennial (12th) Edition

Edited by
Edward Conrad Smith
and
Harold J. Spaeth

BARNES & NOBLE BOOKS

A DIVISION OF HARPER & ROW, PUBLISHERS

New York, Grand Rapids, Philadelphia, St. Louis, San Francisco
London, Singapore, Sydney, Tokyo, Toronto

THE CONSTITUTION OF THE UNITED STATES *(Bicentennial [12th] Edition).* 1936, 1937, 1940, 1949, 1951, 1954, 1955; copyright © 1956, 1966 by Barnes & Noble, Inc. Copyright © 1972, 1975, 1979 by Edward Conrad Smith. Copyright © 1987 by Harper & Row, Publishers, Inc. All rights reserved. Printed in the United States of America. No part of this book may be used or reproduced in any manner whatsoever without written permission except in the case of brief quotations embodied in critical articles and reviews. For information address Harper & Row, Publishers, Inc., 10 East 53rd Street, New York, N.Y. 10022.

Designer: Erich Hobbing
Copy editor: Karen McDermott

Library of Congress Cataloging-in-Publication Data

Smith, Edward Conrad, 1891–
The Constitution of the United States, with case summaries.

(College outline series ; CO/209)
Bibliography: p.
Includes indexes.
1. United States—Constitutional law—Digests. I. Spaeth, Harold J. II. United States. Constitution. 1987. III. Title. IV. Series.
KF4547.7.S6   1987   342.73′029   86-46100
ISBN 0-06-460209-5 (pbk.) 347.30229

90 91 MPC 10 9 8 7 6 5

Contents

★   ★   ★   ★

Contents

Contents

Contents

Preface

★　　　★　　　★　　　★

In 1936, Barnes & Noble published a small paperback book containing complete texts of the Constitution of the United States and the Declaration of Independence, with explanatory notes and charts by William R. Barnes. It was a time of unusual interest in the Constitution because a conservative majority of the Supreme Court was rather systematically declaring important New Deal legislation to be unconstitutional. Since then, interest in the Constitution has remained keen, whetted by such controversies as the proper scope of federal regulatory authority, internal security and the Red scare of the 1950s, the civil rights movement of the 1960s, the revolution in criminal procedure engineered by the Warren Court during its last half-dozen years, and such controversies of the 1970s and 1980s as pornography, abortion, gender discrimination, and affirmative action.

Additional material concerning the development of the Constitution and its amendments has been added in more recent editions of this book. The most extensive revision included summaries of Supreme Court decisions that show how judicial interpretation has developed the meaning of the Constitution. For this edition, these summaries have been rewritten, updated, and reorganized into categories that relate to the issues with which the justices currently struggle. This new material balances and completes the book. Only the most important cases have been summarized—those in which the Supreme Court substantially altered existing constitutional law and established new guidelines for the resolution of future controversies. The cases are succinctly summarized, and readers should keep in mind that many details are omitted. For additional information on these and other decisions, one can consult various treatises, casebooks, and commentaries—a number of which are listed in the selected references section. Nor should one overlook the text of the cases themselves.

This edition, the twelfth, marks the bicentennial of the Constitution, the world's longest-enduring national constitution. It also marks the end of the Burger Court and the beginning of the Rehnquist Court. Unlike the Constitution, the Burger Court is history and the case summaries include decisions from throughout its seventeen-year existence: 1969–1986. Publication of this edition antedates any important decisions of the Rehnquist Court. We do, however, indicate the likely direction the Rehnquist Court will initially take, including that of its newest member, Antonin Scalia.

Nancy Cone, former editor of Barnes & Noble Books, who has had much to do with recent editions of the work, reviewed the new material for this twelfth edition and provided many valuable suggestions. Jeanne Flagg, present editor at Harper & Row, effectively and efficiently directed the project from beginning to end. Karen McDermott copyedited the manuscript with a finely focused eye. Her efforts excised deviations from proper syntax and otherwise enhanced the clarity of murky prose.

Harold J. Spaeth

The Constitution
of the
United States

The Origins
of the Constitution

★　　　★　　　★　　　★

The Constitution of 1787 was the product of seven centuries of development in England and America. The Magna Charta (1215) is as much the heritage of Americans as of Englishmen. So is the common law that limited the authority of the Crown's ministers and governed the Crown's subjects. Colonial legislatures claimed the rights and privileges of Parliament against royal governors. From experience in living under charters in some of the colonies, Americans learned the value of written documents that specified the rights of the people and the powers of government. They frequently made efforts to adapt English institutions to the conditions of a new continent and a relatively classless society.

Disagreement among Americans about the political relationship of the colonies to the mother country produced a breach between them. King George III, his ministers, and the majority party in Parliament regarded the colonies as subordinate to England. Americans believed each colony to be a coequal part of the Crown's dominions and as such entitled to self-government and exempt from parliamentary taxation, legislation, and administrative regulation. They sought to redress their grievances by protests, petitions, nonimportation agreements, and, finally, by resort to arms.

In May 1775, three weeks after the Revolutionary War began at Lexington and Concord, The Second Continental Congress met in Philadelphia. Its members were delegates of patriotic organizations in each of the colonies sent to concert measures for the common defense. The Congress assumed many of the powers of

1

government: it created an army and navy, appointed officers, borrowed money, issued paper currency, and appealed to Europe for help. It adopted the Declaration of Independence, recommended the creation of state constitutions, and drew up the Articles of Confederation, all highly important documents in American constitutional development.

REVOLUTION AND INDEPENDENCE

Though a few radical leaders advocated independence from the beginning, most Americans hoped for reconciliation with Great Britain. On July 6, 1775, the Congress issued the lengthy "Declaration of the Causes and Necessity of Taking Up Arms," which detailed American grievances while explicitly denying any intention to separate from Great Britain and establish independent states. King George replied by proclaiming a state of rebellion in the colonies, and Parliament dutifully passed an act that cut off colonial trade. Moderate leaders now became convinced that independence was the only alternative to submission. Thomas Paine's emotionally charged pamphlet "Common Sense" was widely circulated throughout the colonies and drew thousands of ordinary Americans to the cause of independence. On June 7, 1776, Richard Henry Lee of Virginia proposed the following resolution to the Continental Congress:

> Resolved, That these United Colonies are, and of right ought to be, free and independent States, that they are absolved from all allegiance to the British Crown, and that all political connection between them and the State of Great Britain is, and ought to be, totally dissolved.

Drafting the Declaration. On June 10, the Congress selected five of its ablest members—John Adams, Benjamin Franklin, Thomas Jefferson, Robert R. Livingston, and Roger Sherman—to draft a declaration of independence. Jefferson was the chief author of the draft submitted to the Congress on June 23. The Congress made two or three changes and voted for independence on July 2.

On July 4, John Hancock, president of the Congress, signed the final draft copy. All but one of the other signatures were appended on August 2.

Contents of the Declaration.   The philosophy underlying the Declaration of Independence derives from John Locke's second treatise, *On Civil Government* (1690), which he had written for the avowed purpose of justifying the English revolution of 1688. According to Locke, men had once lived isolated lives in a state of nature. At a certain stage of development they entered into social contracts with one another, thereby creating a society as well as a government. By the terms of the contract each individual surrendered part of his natural rights and in return received protection against other people and other advantages of government. Governmental actions were to accord with moral principles, with the will of the majority determining what was right or wrong. If a government seriously threatened the interests of society, the people might overthrow it and substitute another government in its place. Jefferson omitted specific references to the imaginary state of nature and social contracts, asserting instead that the equality of men and their natural rights were "self-evident."

The Declaration indicts the King and Parliament for usurping power and for tyrannical actions, such as "abolishing our most valuable laws" and "waging war against us." For these and other reasons, the United Colonies declared themselves free and independent states with all the powers rightfully belonging to sovereign states.

Effects of the Declaration.   The Declaration of Independence powerfully stimulated the patriots' cause. It persuasively justified a resort to arms and by implication that American governments would rest on the will of the people. Though it did not immediately result in the emancipation of slaves or in universal suffrage, abolitionists and suffragettes effectively used the egalitarian principles of the Declaration to advance their causes. It continues to prod the American conscience today to improve the conditions of various minorities.

STATE CONSTITUTIONS

Beginning in 1776, revolutionary assemblies in most states formulated written constitutions, using colonial charters as models. All of them had certain common features.

Popular Sovereignty. The people were declared to be the source of governmental authority. In the words of the Georgia constitution of 1777: "We, therefore, the representatives of the people, from whom all power originates and for whose benefit all government is intended, by virtue of the power delegated to us, do ordain ... that the following rules and regulations be adopted for the future government of this state." The Massachusetts constitution of 1780 expressed the same idea in the form of an original social contract: "The whole people convenants with each citizen, and each citizen with the whole people, that all shall be governed by certain laws for the common good."

Eclipse of the Executive. Executive power in the states entered an eclipse that lasted until the adoption of the Constitution of the United States. Pennsylvania's first constitution did not even provide for a governor. In ten states the governor's term was just one year and his administrative powers were few. Only New York gave the governor sufficient power and a long enough term (three years) to enable him to be an effective chief executive.

Legislative Supremacy. In a majority of the states the legislature elected the governor, judges, and other officers and determined the policies of government. It possessed lawmaking, financial, and supervisory powers. As the successor of Parliament, the legislature was considered to hold general residual authority: it could exercise any power not granted to another governmental body. Except in Pennsylvania and Georgia, the legislature comprised two houses. In most states, its members were chosen by voters who owned considerable property.

Limited Government. The most remarkable state document of this period is the bill of rights prefixed to the Virginia constitution of 1776. George Mason wrote the first fifteen articles; Patrick Henry wrote the sixteenth article, on religious freedom. The

Virginia Bill of Rights states the principles on which all branches of government, including the legislature, should operate and guaranteed individual liberties. It influenced the writing of later constitutions both in the United States and in Europe.

THE CONFEDERATION OF THE STATES

The same Virginia resolution that proposed independence called on Congress to prepare a plan for a confederation of the states. On July 12, 1776, debate began on a draft written by John Dickinson; it continued whenever time could be spared from urgent military matters. Unfortunately, the concerns of the individual states outweighed considerations of national interest. States with claims to western lands refused to grant Congress power to settle boundary disputes. The small states insisted on amendments to ensure their sovereignty, while the large states tried (in vain) to apportion voting strength in Congress according to population or the amount that each state contributed to the common fund. The Southern states insisted on apportioning expenses of the Confederation according to the value of land in private hands rather than on the basis of total population including slaves. Not until November 1, 1777, did Congress submit the Articles to the states for ratification.

Most of the states ratified them fairly promptly, but Maryland, expressing fears for its future among powerful neighbors, held out until other states agreed to cede their western lands to the United States. The Articles became effective on March 1, 1781.

Structure of the Confederation. The Articles variously described the new arrangement as a "confederacy," as a "firm league of friendship," and as a "perpetual Union." It was less a government than an agency that made possible cooperation among the state governments. Each state retained its sovereignty, freedom, and independence. To amend the Articles required unanimous approval of the state legislatures. No article provided for an executive or a permanent judiciary. The chief organ of government was a Congress composed of delegates annually chosen from each state. Each state paid its own delegation and could recall them at will. Each delegation cast one vote, and any important action required the approval of nine states. The Articles did provide, however, for cooperation among the states, including a full faith and credit clause and a privileges and immunities clause. Several limitations on state action that were expressed in Article VI were later carried over into the Constitution of the United States, as were many of the powers granted to Congress in Article IX. The fatal defects of the Articles were what they omitted. They did not provide for a vigorous executive. Congress had no control over commerce between the states and with foreign countries. It had no power to tax and could only "requisition" states to provide necessary revenue. The states were to levy appropriate taxes and remit the proceeds. Finally, Congress could not exert any of its limited powers over individuals.

The Confederation Period.   Unsettled economic conditions at the close of the Revolution severely tested both the state governments and Congress. In some states the legislatures yielded to the demands of debtors and issued large quantities of paper money or enacted "stay laws" postponing the dates when debtors were legally obliged to pay their creditors. In violation of the Articles, some states imposed tariffs or other trade barriers preventing the free flow of commerce from other states. In varying degrees states failed to meet their financial obligations to the Confederation. Of a total of $10 million requisitioned by Congress, only $1.5 million was actually paid; one state paid nothing at all. Largely because of Congress' inability to meet interest payments, the public debt increased after the Revolution ended. The Confederation maintained only a small army, 750 officers and men, for the defense of the United States against Indians and other potential enemies. With the Ordinances of 1785 and 1787, Congress established fundamental and durable policies for the survey of public lands and the government of territories, but it was unable to promote much settlement in the Northwest Territory. Though the country's ablest leaders engaged in diplomacy, they were singularly unsuccessful in negotiating commercial treaties, in part because foreign nations feared that the states would not fullfill the treaty obligations of the United States.

Failure of the Amending Process. In 1781, Congress proposed an amendment to the Articles that would enable it to levy a duty of 5 percent on all imported goods. All the states ratified the amendment except Rhode Island. Twelve states ratified a second amendment designed to meet Rhode Island's objections, but this time New York refused to give its approval despite Congress' warning that without revenues the Confederation would disintegrate. Both Rhode Island and New York possessed fine harbors that served as ports of entry for the trade of nearby states, and both were unwilling to surrender part of their tariff duties for the common good. The position of Rhode Island and New York made it plain that if the Union were to be strengthened, other means would have to be employed than the cumbrous procedure in the Articles.

THE MOVEMENT FOR A NEW CONSTITUTION

A number of groups combined to create the Constitution of the United States. Among the most important were former officers of the Continental Army and former members of Congress who, in the course of their service, had developed national loyalties; leaders from the large states of Virginia, Pennsylvania, and Massachusetts who believed that the power of one state to prevent change endangered the future of all the states; leaders from the small states of Connecticut, New Jersey, and Delaware who sought to overcome the commercial restrictions of New York and Pennsylvania; Georgians who wanted national help against an Indian war that threatened; and merchants and shipowners in all the states. Leaders included Alexander Hamilton of New York, who as military secretary to George Washington had observed the weakness and incapacity of Congress, and James Madison, an associate of Thomas Jefferson and opponent of Patrick Henry in Virginia politics.

Call for the Convention. In 1785 commissioners from Virginia and Maryland amicably settled boundary disputes, navigation rights on Chesapeake Bay, and tariff duties. When the Maryland commissioners proposed a larger conference, which would include Delaware and Pennsylvania, the Virginia legislature seized the opportunity to call a meeting of delegates from all the states at Annapolis in September 1786. Nine states responded by appointing delegates, but only five states were represented when the conference convened because the delegates from four states failed to reach the convention site, Annapolis, in time to participate. Those present adopted a strongly worded report, supposedly written by Hamilton, stressing the deficiencies in the existing government and calling for a convention of delegates from all the states to meet in Philadelphia on May 14, 1787, for the purpose of "digesting a Plan" for remedying the defects in the Articles of Confederation. After several states had chosen delegates, Congress issued a formal call for a convention "for the sole and express purpose of revising the Articles of Confederation."

Selection of Delegates. The Virginia legislature chose an able delegation, including Washington, who was persuaded to come out of retirement, James Madison, George Mason, and Governor Edmund Randolph. Pennsylvania sent the largest delegation: it included Franklin, whose reputation was surpassed only by Washington's; James Wilson, who had consistently asserted that the Americans were one people; and Gouverneur Morris, a brilliant New Yorker temporarily residing in Philadelphia. Although the New York legislature designated Hamilton as a delegate, it also took care to send with him John Lansing and Robert Yates, members of the state's dominant anti-Federalist party. The New Hampshire legislature chose delegates but neglected to provide for their expenses; they arrived in late July—after Lansing and Yates of the New York delegation had left the convention. Rhode Island alone appointed no delegates. Other outstanding members of the Constitutional Convention included Rufus King and Elbridge Gerry of Massachusetts, Roger Sherman and William Samuel Johnson of Connecticut, and John Rutledge and the two Pinckneys of South Carolina.

Of the fifty-five delegates who attended the convention, thirty-nine had served in Congress, and all were experienced in the politics of their states. A large number were young men, in their early thirties; the average age was about forty-three. Among those not in attendance were Jefferson and John Adams, who were serving abroad as ministers to France and Great Britain, respectively. Patrick Henry and a number of other leaders who were primarily interested in state politics declined to participate.

THE CONVENTION OF 1787

Only the Virginia and Pennsylvania delegations arrived in Philadelphia at the appointed time; not until May 25 could the convention be convened because of transportation problems. The delegates unanimously elected Washington as presiding officer. Rules of procedure provided each state delegation with one vote. The delegates agreed to keep their deliberations secret, an action that is partly responsible for the theory—now generally discredited—that they engaged in an undemocratic conspiracy to undo the work of the Revolution, by replacing the Articles with a centralized government that would undermine state sovereignty. The closed sessions enabled the participants to express opinions freely, to advance tentative proposals, to reconsider decisions without being publicly chastised for inconsistency, and to negotiate, bargain, and compromise. They determined to prepare a comprehensive document and to be judged on their work as a whole.

Records of the Convention. Madison, sensing the historical importance of the convention, obtained its permission to take notes on the debates. Other members sometimes helped by giving him copies or outlines of their remarks. Madison's notes, which were not published until 1840, four years after his death, constitute practically the only dependable source of information concerning the debates. The recollections of other delegates, written after the convention had adjourned, supplement them in part.

The Virginia Plan. After arriving in Philadelphia, the Virginia delegation drafted a series of resolutions to serve as a basis for discussion. Their proposal provided for the supremacy of the legislative branch, a national executive, and a system of national courts. The legislature would consist of two houses, one of which would be elected by popular vote and the other selected by the first house from persons nominated by the state legislatures. A state's voting strength in each house would be proportionate to the taxes paid by the state or to the number of its free inhabitants. The legislature would have the power to enact laws on all matters in which the separate states were incompetent, to void state laws contravening the constitution, to use the military forces of the Union against any recalcitrant state, and to elect the national executive and the judges of national courts.

The delegates debated the Virginia plan for two weeks, making a number of changes. They agreed that representatives in the lower house should be apportioned according to population and—by a margin of one vote—that the same apportionment should apply to the second house. The delegation from New Jersey requested an adjournment in order to prepare a different plan.

The New Jersey Plan.   On June 15, William Paterson of New Jersey introduced resolutions that the Convention only propose amendments to the Articles of Confederation as Congress had specified. He suggested that Congress be given power to levy duties on goods imported into the United States, to impose a tax on documents, and to regulate the collection of both. If additional revenues were needed, Congress would not only requisition the states but also collect taxes in noncomplying states. Congress would have power to regulate foreign and interstate commerce. All laws of Congress and all treaties made under the authority of the United States would be the supreme law of the respective states. Congress would choose a plural executive, with general authority to execute federal acts, appoint federal officers, and direct all military operations. A supreme court appointed by the executive with jurisdiction on appeal over cases arising from the construction of treaties, the regulation of trade, and the collection of revenue was also proposed.

If the New Jersey plan had been formulated before the Convention met, it would have been satisfactory to all but the most dedicated nationalists. But only New York and Delaware supported it. Furthermore, many provisions of the Virginia plan, especially the apportionment of the upper house according to population, required alteration to gain support from the smaller states.

The Great Compromise.   At this point the lines between the large and small states became tightly drawn, and talk of adjourning the convention was heard. Large-state delegates insisted that representation be based on population; the small states feared to enter a union dominated by the large states. Besides, they argued, their residents would never accept a constitution that did not recognize the principle of state equality. After three weeks of recrimination, the delegates agreed to the Great (sometimes called the Connecticut) Compromise: a lower house chosen according to population and with the sole authority to originate revenue bills, and an upper house in which each state would have an equal vote.

Compromise of Sectional Interests.   Northern commercial interests wanted Congress to have the power to regulate interstate commerce, while the South opposed duties on exports. In addition to free exportation of their commodities, Southern delegates also demanded that Congress have no power to interfere with the slave trade. The compromise finally reached provided, in return for congressional power over interstate commerce, that exports would not be taxed and that the slave trade could continue until 1808.

The formula for apportioning representatives and direct taxes counted a slave as three-fifths of a free person.

Powers of Congress.   Most of the delegates considered the broad grant of federal powers in the Virginia plan impractical. To disallow state laws would cause resentment, and the use of military force would amount to making war on a state. Instead, the delegates decided to enumerate the specific powers that Congress might exercise. The Committee on Detail compiled a list, taking most of the powers—some of them verbatim—from the Articles of Confederation and adding others from various state constitutions. The tax power remained broadly stated except concerning direct taxes. Congress received a choice of means to carry out its enumerated powers at the end of Article I, section 8 of the Constitution in the "necessary and proper" clause.

The Executive Article.   Nothing gave the convention more trouble than the creation of an adequately empowered executive who would be accountable to the electorate. The delegates debated the merits of a plural as opposed to a single executive. They considered tenure for life and for a single seven-year term before settling on a four-year term with the opportunity for reelection. In provisions borrowed from the constitution of New York, the convention created a strong executive, but they made him subject to impeachment and trial by Congress. As to presidential selection, the convention discarded legislative election, because it would make the president subservient to Congress, and also popular election, because it would give excessive weight to the populous states. The result was an electoral college weighted in favor of the small states. The least populous state would have three electors, while a state with ten times as many people would have only four times as many electors. If no candidate received a majority of the electoral college vote, the House of Representatives, voting by states and with each state having one vote, would select from among the five highest candidates. Washington was expected to be the first president, serving as many terms as he desired. After his administration, the delegates thought that the electoral vote would be divided among many candidates, throwing the election into the House, where the small states, being in the majority, would choose the president.

The Judiciary Article.   The convention agreed early on to create a supreme court and to provide federal judges with tenure. Sharp differences did arise over whether to create a separate set of lower federal courts or to provide for the trial of federal cases in courts of the various states. The delegates astutely resolved the issue by authorizing Congress to create inferior federal courts if it so desired. The Supreme Court received original jurisdiction to decide cases involving foreign diplomatic and consular officers and to resolve disputes between states. Federal judges were to be appointed by the president with the consent of the Senate.

The Supremacy Clause. In Article VI of the Constitution, a provision that first appeared in the New Jersey plan declared that laws made in accordance with the Constitution and treaties would be the supreme law of the land. State judges were bound to uphold the supremacy of federal law even if it conflicted with state constitutions or laws. Another clause designed to strengthen the Union required state legislative, executive, and judicial officers to take an oath to support the Constitution of the United States.

Position of the States under the Constitution. The federal government guarantees to each state a republican form of government, protection from invasion, and, at its request, protection from domestic violence. No state can be divided, merged with another state, or be deprived of its equal vote in the Senate without its own consent. The Constitution says nothing about state sovereignty. The states may not coin money, issue paper money, make anything but gold and silver coin a legal tender in payment of debts, pass any law impairing the obligation of contracts, levy taxes on imports or exports, or, without the consent of Congress, enter into a compact with another state. These prohibitions addressed concerns of financial and business interests about laws enacted by various states during the confederation period. In order to promote harmonious relations with one another, the states must give full faith and credit to the public acts, records, and judicial decisions of other states; treat citizens of other states as they do their own residents; and return fugitives from justice and runaway slaves to the states from which they had fled.

Democratic Basis of the Constitution. The preamble of the Articles of Confederation named the states in order from north to south. How was the Convention to enumerate the participating states without knowing which would ratify? In a brilliant flash of inspiration, the delegates began the Constitution with the words, "We the people of the United States . . . do ordain and establish this Constitution . . ."

Method of Ratification. The members of the Constitutional Convention considered ratification by state conventions composed of specially elected delegates more likely than ratification by the state legislatures. The legislatures would not view kindly an instrument of government that would reduce their own powers. Given the opposition of New York and Rhode Island, the convention abandoned all thought of requiring every state to ratify it. Because of anti-Federalist sentiment, the delegates decided that the Constitution should go into effect when nine states ratified it.

Amending Procedure. The delegates recognized that changing circumstances and conditions might flaw the Constitution after it took effect; they therefore determined not to continue the disastrous amending procedure of the Articles of Confederation. They first voted to permit Congress to call a convention to propose amendments at the request of two thirds of the states. As the Convention moved toward adjournment, they added an alternative method: a two thirds vote of both houses of Congress. The alternative means of ratification paralleled the choice of methods to propose amendments: the legislatures of or conventions in three fourths of the states.

Guarantees of Rights. The original Constitution contains several important guarantees of individual rights: the writ of habeas corpus and prohibition of bills of attainder and ex post facto laws in Article I, section 9; trial by jury and a narrow definition of treason in Article III; and a prohibition of religious tests as a condition for holding federal office in Article VI. A formal list of other rights was considered either too difficult to specify or unnecessary. A proposal late in the session to appoint a committee to draft a bill of rights failed badly.

End of the Session. A committee on style arranged in logical order the provisions previously approved. Gouverneur Morris apparently wrote the final draft. Only thirty-nine of the fifty-five members who attended at least some of the sessions signed the Constitution; such major participants as Eldridge Gerry of Massachusetts and George Mason and Edmund Randolph of Virginia for various reasons refused to sign. On September 17, the Convention adjourned after nearly four months of being in virtually continuous session.

Political Theory of the Constitution. Although Madison and others had studied the history of previous federations, they had formulated no hard-and-fast theories on the subject. Their attitude was pragmatic. Every constitutional provision was based on experience in the states, the colonies, or Britain. The powers delegated to the federal government were determined by what was needed and what the state conventions might accept. For theoretical inspiration they relied on John Locke and on Montesquieu's *Spirit of the Laws*. Both writers had insisted on the need to separate powers in order to prevent tyranny; in Montesquieu's view even the people's representatives in the legislature could not be trusted. The delegates therefore specified the powers of each branch in a separate article and devised ingenious checks and balances to make cooperation among the legislative, executive, and judicial branches even more difficult. Although the Constitution makes no mention of Locke's state of nature or his original contract, it derives its authority from the will of the people—as the preamble and Article VII indicate. To people familiar with Locke's theories, the Constitution created a latter-day social contract.

THE CONTEST OVER RATIFICATION

The convention sent copies of the Constitution to Congress, which transmitted them without comment to the states. More or less promptly (except in Rhode Island) the legislatures arranged for the selection of delegates to conventions. In the contest over ratification, the federalists, though a minority, had the advantage of unity, initiative, and a novel and interesting proposal. The opposition was divided, overconfident, and badly led.

Discussions in the Press. The text of the Constitution and arguments for and against its adoption occupied much of the space in American newspapers during the ensuing months. The most noteworthy series of articles supporting ratification was written by Hamilton, Madison, and John Jay for New York newspapers. Their masterful essays formulated a theory of maximum liberty and governmental effectiveness through federalism and refuted the objections of the antifederalists on theoretical and practical grounds. *The Federalist Papers* (as the collected articles were later called) remains the best theoretical justification of the American constitutional system.

Richard Henry Lee's series "Letters of the Federal Farmer" perhaps best exemplified the antifederalist position. He characterized the new system of government as "calculated ultimately to make the states one consolidated government." He warned that adoption of the Constitution might result in abolition of the laws, customs, and constitutions of the states. He argued that the proposed House of Representatives would not be sufficiently responsive to the wishes of the people and objected to the absence of a bill of rights to protect individual liberties. Other antifederalists, taking a narrow legalistic approach, argued that the convention had exceeded its authority, since it had been called only to propose amendments to the Articles of Confederation. They demanded to know by what authority the convention had used the phrase "We the people," since the states were the parties to the compact that had created the Articles of Confederation. On practical grounds some antifederalists asserted that a federal government could not effectively exert power over so large a territory as the United States; others feared that its capital would become, as London had, a center of concentrated power. Few clauses in the proposed constitution escaped criticism.

Ratification of the Constitution.   By mid-January 1788, five state conventions had ratified the Constitution—Delaware, New Jersey, and Georgia unanimously, Connecticut and Pennsylvania by votes of two or three to one. Maryland approved it on April 28 and South Carolina on May 23 by overwhelming majorities. Intense opposition was encountered in the other six states. When the Massachusetts convention met in January, preliminary votes showed a majority of the delegates opposed to the Constitution; they were led by Gerry, Samuel Adams, and John Hancock. After heated discussion, the opposition yielded when supporters agreed to recommend antifederalist amendments to the Constitution. Massachusetts ratified it by a narrow vote on February 6. In New Hampshire, the federalists avoided defeat in January by procuring a long adjournment. After a bitter struggle, they won out on June 21, and New Hampshire became the ninth state to ratify. Four days later, the Virginia federalists, under the leadership of Madison and John Marshall, overcame an early disadvantage, despite the efforts of George Mason, Patrick Henry, and Richard Henry Lee. In New York, the antifederalists had a two-to-one advantage, but news of New Hampshire's and Virginia's ratification turned the tide. By a margin of three votes, New York ratified the Constitution on July 26, 1788. The new government commenced operations on April 30, 1789. North Carolina entered the Union the following November and Rhode Island more than a year later.

In the state conventions, the federalists' main strength came from representatives of shipowners, merchants, and artisans in the towns near the Atlantic coast and from frontiersmen. These groups felt the need for more adequate foreign and military policies and an end to interstate trade barriers. Opposition to the Constitution was strongest in up-country agricultural areas where the principal needs were better roads and courthouse services, both of which state and local governments could supply. In varying degrees, antifederalist attitudes were determined by state and local political alignments, vague fears of a federal colossus, and the conviction, held especially in New York and Rhode Island, that establishment of the federal government would increase taxes on land and other property. In the debates over ratification, the most criticized feature of the Constitution was the lack of a bill of rights. The federalists mollified the opposition by promising to add a bill of rights through the amendment process. They were not obliged to yield on any other point.

CHANGES IN THE CONSTITUTION BY AMENDMENT

On June 8, 1789, in accordance with federalist promises James Madison introduced a number of proposed amendments in the House of Representatives. He intended them to be inserted at appropriate places in the text of the Constitution, but Roger Sherman of Connecticut persuaded Congress to add them at the end, so that each amendment would stand or fall on its own merits when submitted to the states for ratification. Congress decided that the president's signature to a proposed amendment was not required. On no occasion have two thirds of the states asked Congress to call a constitutional convention. Congress has proposed all amendments, determined their exact phraseology, and sometimes fixed a limit of seven years within which the amendment must be ratified. Except for the Twenty-first Amendment, which repealed Prohibtion, state legislatures ratified all the others. Once a legislature has ratified an amendment, neither it nor the voters of the state in a referendum may rescind the ratification. But the same or a later legislature may ratify an amendment after previous failures to ratify. The Twenty-first Amendment was referred to state conventions in order to obtain the opinion of bodies especially chosen for the purpose of determining whether or not to retain Prohibition.

The Bill of Rights. The first ten amendments are called the Bill of Rights. Their contents derive from English and colonial experience and from the political thought and experience of the Revolutionary and Confederation periods.

The First Amendment prohibits the establishment of a state-supported church, requires the separation of church and state, and guarantees freedom of worship, of speech, and the press and the right to peaceably assemble and petition the government. On occasion, the Supreme Court has treated the provisions of the First Amendment as more fundamental than other parts of the Constitution. Indeed, a few justices have considered them as virtually absolute. On the other hand, the Court has upheld substantial limitations on the exercise of the First Amendment during wartime and when the public has feared subversion.

The Second and Third Amendments reflect the framers' concerns about a standing army and soldiers billeted in private households.

The Fourth to the Eighth Amendments pertain to the protection of life, liberty, and property. Most of their provisions are designed to protect citizens from improper conduct by the police and to establish fair procedures in collecting evidence and in the arrest, indictment, and trial of individuals. These amendments prohibit unreasonable searches and seizures, the use of illegally obtained evidence compelling someone to incriminate himself, involuntary confessions, denial of reasonable bail, double jeopardy, unduly delayed or unfair trials, and cruel or unusual punishment. Accused persons have the right to be informed of the charges against them, to confront their accusers in open court, and to have the court's help in compelling the attendance of witnesses to testify on their behalf. The requirement of due process of law (equivalent to the English "law of the land") governs the interpretation of these and other matters, including the judge's fairness in conducting the trial and instructing the jury. The due process clause also protects property rights against impairment by legislation in excess of Congress' powers, as well as from unfair acts and procedures by executive and administrative officers, quasi-legislative commissions, and courts of law.

The Ninth Amendment reassured the public that the enumeration of rights in the Constitution was not exhaustive and did not preclude the existence and enforcement of others.

The Tenth Amendment limits the centralizing tendencies of government. When it was proposed, antifederalists made a determined but unsuccessful effort to confine the federal government to expressly granted powers and to reserve all other powers to the states or to the people thereof. As adopted, the amendment leaves the principle of implied federal powers intact and acknowledges the existence of undefined powers belonging to the public at large.

Later Amendments. The Eleventh Amendment prohibits a nonresident from suing a state in the federal courts. It was adopted in response to states' rights sentiments after the Supreme Court took jurisdiction of a case (*Chisholm* v. *Georgia*) in which South Carolina creditors sued Georgia to recover confiscated property.

The Twelfth Amendment recognized the effect of political parties on the election process. In the election of 1800, all the Republican members of the electoral college—each of whom could cast two votes for president—gave one vote to Jefferson and the other to Aaron Burr, the party's nominees for president and vice president respectively. The resulting tie caused the election to devolve upon the House of Representatives, which the federalists controlled. Before Jefferson was finally chosen, much partisan maneuvering to elect Burr president had transpired. To prevent a similar situation from recurring, the Twelfth Amendment requires each elector to designate separately his or her choice for president and vice president.

The Thirteenth Amendment constitutionalized Lincoln's Emancipation Proclamation and freed all slaves (mostly those in border states) who had not been included in the Proclamation. The phrase "involuntary servitude" outlaws peonage or forced labor under contract.

The Fourteenth Amendment rejected Southern doctrines of state sovereignty and secession and overrode the Supreme Court's decision in *Scott* v. *Sandford,* which held that no black person could be an American citizen. The due process and equal protection clauses safeguard civil rights and liberties from state impairment. For many years the Supreme Court used the due process clause to insulate business from state regulation. But beginning with *Gitlow* v. *New York* (1925), the Court gradually expanded its definition of due process to include most of the noneconomic guarantees in the Bill of Rights and thereby protect them from state impairment. A similar development occurred with respect to the equal protection clause. In *Plessy* v. *Ferguson* (1896), the Court upheld the constitutionality of "separate but equal" public facilities. Subsequently, the Court held governmentally mandated segregation to be inherently unequal in *Brown* v. *Board of Education* (1954).

The Fifteenth Amendment forbids the states to deny a person the right to vote because of race, color, or previous condition of servitude. Southern states, however, used the failure to pay a poll tax and unfairly administered literacy tests to prevent blacks from voting until the mid-1960s.

The Sixteenth Amendment overrides the Supreme Court's decision in *Pollock* v. *Farmers' Loan & Trust Co.* (1895), which held that a tax on incomes derived from property was a direct tax, and empowers Congress to impose an income tax without apportionment among the states, as Article I, section 9, of the Constitution had required.

The Seventeenth Amendment requires that United States Senators be popularly elected instead of chosen by the legislatures of the various states.

The Eighteenth Amendment prohibited the manufacture, sale, or transportation of intoxicating liquors and gave Congress and the state legislatures concurrent power to enforce the amendment.

The Nineteenth Amendment forbids a state to deny suffrage because of sex, thus enfranchising women on the same terms as men.

The Twentieth Amendment moves the beginning of congressional sessions from March 4 to January 3 and of presidential terms to January 20. A newly elected Congress must meet January 3, two months after its election, instead of eleven months afterward.

The Twenty-first Amendment repeals the Eighteenth.

The Twenty-second Amendment limits the president to two terms in office, thereby constitutionalizing the customary limitation that had existed from the end of Washington's second term until the election of Franklin D. Roosevelt to a third and fourth term.

The Twenty-third Amendment enables the voters of the District of Columbia to elect as many presidential electors as the district would be entitled to if it were a state, but not more than the least populous state.

The Twenty-fourth Amendment forbids denying a person the right to vote in any federal election because of failure to pay a poll or any other tax. (The Supreme Court subsequently declared the poll tax requirement in state elections unconstitutional in *Harper* v. *Virginia State Board of Elections* [1966].)

The Twenty-fifth Amendment provides that the vice president shall become acting president whenever the president states that he is unable to perform his duties or a similar statement is made by a body authorized by Congress to determine if the president is unable to perform his duties. If the president asserts his competence, Congress must decide the matter within twenty-one days and, by a two thirds vote of both houses, may declare the president unable to perform his duties.

The Twenty-sixth Amendment extends suffrage in both state and national elections to all citizens who are eighteen years of age. It was adopted after the Supreme Court, in *Oregon* v. *Mitchell* (1970), declared the provisions of the Voting Rights Act of 1965 unconstitutional insofar as they related to state elections.

Documents

*   *   *   *

VIRGINIA BILL OF RIGHTS*

Adopted June 12, 1776

A declaration of rights made by the representatives of the good people of Virginia, assembled in full and free convention; which rights do pertain to them and their posterity, as the basis and foundation of government.

SECTION 1. That all men are by nature equally free and independent, and have certain inherent rights, of which, when they enter into a state of society, they cannot, by any compact, deprive or divest their posterity; namely, the enjoyment of life and liberty, with the means of acquiring and possessing property, and pursuing and obtaining happiness and safety.

SECTION 2. That all power is vested in, and consequently derived from, the people; that magistrates are their trustees and servants, and at all times amenable to them.

SECTION 3. That government is, or ought to be, instituted for the common benefit, protection, and security of the people, nation, or community; of all the various modes and forms of government, that is best which is capable of producing the greatest degree of happiness and safety, and is most effectually secured against the danger of maladministration; and that, when any government shall be found inadequate or contrary to these purposes, a majority of the community hath an indubitable, inalienable, and infeasible

*B. P. Poore, ed., *The Federal and States Constitutions, Colonial Charters, and Other Organic Laws of the United States* (2nd ed., Washington, D.C.: Government Printing Office, 1878), II, 1908 ff.

right to reform, alter, or abolish it, in such manner as shall be judged most conducive to the public weal.

SECTION 4.   That no man, or set of men, are entitled to exclusive or separate emoluments or privileges from the community, but in consideration of public services; which, not being descendible, neither ought the offices of magistrate, legislator, or judge to be hereditary.

SECTION 5.   That the legislative and executive powers of the State should be separate and distinct from the judiciary; and that the members of the two first may be restrained from oppression, by feeling and participating the burdens of the people, they should, at fixed periods, be reduced to a private station, return into that body from which they were originally taken, and the vacancies be supplied by frequent, certain, and regular elections, in which all, or any part of the former members, to be again eligible, or ineligible, as the laws shall direct.

SECTION 6.   That elections of members to serve as representatives of the people in assembly, ought to be free; and that all men, having sufficient evidence of permanent common interest with, and attachment to, the community, have the right of suffrage, and cannot be taxed or deprived of their property for public uses, without their own consent, or that of their representatives so elected, nor bound by any law to which they have not, in like manner, assented, for the public good.

SECTION 7.   That all power of suspending laws, or the execution of laws, by any authority, without consent of the representatives of the people, is injurious to their rights, and ought not to be exercised.

SECTION 8.   That in all capital or criminal prosecutions a man hath a right to demand the cause and nature of his accusation, to be confronted with the accusers and witnesses, to call for evidence in his favor, and to a speedy trial by an impartial jury of twelve men of his vicinage, without whose unanimous consent he cannot be found guilty; nor can he be compelled to give evidence against himself; that no man be deprived of his liberty, except by the law of the land or the judgment of his peers.

SECTION 9. That excessive bail ought not to be required, nor excessive fines imposed, nor cruel and unusual punishment inflicted.

SECTION 10. That general warrants, whereby an officer or messenger may be commanded to search suspected places without evidence of a fact committed, or to seize any person or persons not named, or whose offence is not particularly described and supported by evidence, are grievous and oppressive, and ought not to be granted.

SECTION 11. That in controversies respecting property, and in suits between man and man, the ancient trial by jury is preferable to any other, and ought to be held sacred.

SECTION 12. That the freedom of the press is one of the great bulwarks of liberty, and can never be restrained but by despotic governments.

SECTION 13. That a well-regulated militia, composed of the body of the people, trained to arms, is the proper, natural, and safe defence of a free State; that standing armies, in time of peace, should be avoided, as dangerous to liberty; and that in all cases the military should be under strict subordination to, and governed by, the civil power.

SECTION 14. That the people have a right to uniform government; and, therefore, that no government separate from, or independent of the government of Virginia, ought to be erected or established within the limits thereof.

SECTION 15. That no free government, or the blessings of liberty, can be preserved to any people, but by a firm adherence to justice, moderation, temperance, frugality, and virtue, and by frequent recurrence to fundamental principles.

SECTION 16. That religion, or the duty which we owe to our Creator, and the manner of discharging it, can be directed only by reason and conviction, not by force or violence; and therefore all men are equally entitled to the free exercise of religion, according to the dictates of conscience; and that it is the mutual duty of all to practise Christian forbearance, love, and charity towards each other.

A DECLARATION

by the Representatives of the
United States of America
in General Congress Assembled
July 4, 1776

When, in the course of human events, it becomes necessary for one people to dissolve the political bands which have connected them with another, and to assume, among the powers of the earth, the separate and equal station to which the laws of nature and of nature's God entitle them, a decent respect to the opinions of mankind requires that they should declare the causes which impel them to the separation.

We hold these truths to be self-evident, that all men are created equal; that they are endowed by their Creator with certain inalienable rights; that among these, are life, liberty, and the pursuit of happiness. That, to secure these rights, governments are instituted among men, deriving their just powers from the consent of the governed; that, whenever any form of government becomes destructive of these ends, it is the right of the people to alter or to abolish it, and to institute a new government, laying its foundation on such principles, and organizing its powers in such form, as to them shall seem most likely to effect their safety and happiness. Prudence, indeed, will dictate that governments long established, should not be changed for light and transient causes; and, accordingly, all experience hath shown, that mankind are more disposed to suffer, while evils are sufferable, than to right themselves by abolishing the forms to which they are accustomed. But, when a long train of abuses and usurpations, pursuing invariably the same object, evinces a design to reduce them under absolute despotism, it is their right, it is their duty, to throw off such government and to provide new guards for their future security. Such has been the patient sufferance of these colonies, and such is now the necessity which constrains them to alter their former systems of government. The history of the present King of Great Britain is a history of repeated injuries and usurpations, all having, in direct object, the establishment of an absolute tyranny over these States. To prove this, let facts be submitted to a candid world:—

He has refused his assent to laws the most wholesome and necessary for the public good.

He has forbidden his governors to pass laws of immediate and pressing importance, unless suspended in their operation till his assent should be obtained; and, when so suspended, he has utterly neglected to attend to them.

He has refused to pass other laws for the accommodation of large districts of people, unless those people would relinquish the right of representation in the legislature: a right inestimable to them, and formidable to tyrants only.

He has called together legislative bodies at places unusual, uncomfortable, and distant from the depository of their public records, for the sole purpose of fatiguing them into compliance with his measures.

He has dissolved representative houses repeatedly for opposing, with manly firmness, his invasions on the rights of the people.

He has refused, for a long time after such dissolutions, to cause others to be elected; whereby the legislative powers, incapable of annihilation, have returned to the people at large for their exercise; the state remaining, in the meantime, exposed to all the danger of invasion from without, and convulsions within.

He has endeavored to prevent the population of these States; for that purpose, obstructing the laws for naturalization of foreigners, refusing to pass others to encourage their migration hither, and raising the conditions of new appropriations of lands.

He has obstructed the administration of justice, by refusing his assent to laws for establishing judiciary powers.

He has made judges dependent on his will alone, for the tenure of their offices, and the amount and payment of their salaries.

He has erected a multitude of new offices, and sent hither swarms of officers, to harass our people, and eat out their substance.

He has kept among us, in time of peace, standing armies, without the consent of our legislatures.

He has affected to render the military independent of, and superior to, the civil power.

He has combined, with others, to subject us to a jurisdiction foreign to our Constitution, and unacknowledged by our laws; giving his assent to their acts of pretended legislation:

For quartering large bodies of armed troops among us:

For protecting them by a mock trial, from punishment, for any murders which they should commit on the inhabitants of these States:

For cutting off our trade with all parts of the world:

For imposing taxes on us without our consent:

For depriving us, in many cases, of the benefit of trial by jury:

For transporting us beyond seas to be tried for pretended offenses:

For abolishing the free system of English laws in a neighboring province, establishing therein an arbitrary government, and enlarging its boundaries, so as to render it at once an example and fit instrument for introducing the same absolute rule into these colonies:

For taking away our charters, abolishing our most valuable laws, and altering, fundamentally, the powers of our governments:

For suspending our own legislatures, and declaring themselves invested with power to legislate for us in all cases whatsoever.

He has abdicated government here, by declaring us out of his protection, and waging war against us.

He has plundered our seas, ravaged our coasts, burnt our towns, and destroyed the lives of our people.

He is, at this time, transporting large armies of foreign mercenaries to complete the works of death, desolation, and tyranny, already begun, with circumstances of cruelty and perfidy scarcely paralleled in the most barbarous ages, and totally unworthy the head of a civilized nation.

He has constrained our fellow citizens, taken captive on the high seas, to bear arms against their country, to become the executioners of their friends, and brethren, or to fall themselves by their hands.

He has excited domestic insurrections amongst us, and has endeavored to bring on the inhabitants of our frontiers, the merciless Indian savages, whose known rule of warfare is an undistinguished destruction of all ages, sexes, and conditions.

In every stage of these oppressions, we have petitioned for redress, in the most humble terms; our repeated petitions have been answered only by repeated injury. A prince, whose character is thus marked by every act which may define a tyrant, is unfit to be the ruler of a free people.

Nor have we been wanting in attention to our British brethren. We have warned them, from time to time, of attempts made by their legislature to extend an unwarrantable jurisdiction over us. We have reminded them of the circumstances of our emigration and settlement here. We have appealed to their native justice and magnanimity, and we have conjured them, by the ties of our common kindred, to disavow these usurpations, which would inevitably interrupt our connections and correspondence. They, too, have been deaf to the voice of justice and consanguinity. We must, therefore, acquiesce in the necessity which denounces our separation, and hold them, as we hold the rest of mankind, enemies in war, in peace, friends.

We, therefore, the representatives of the United States of America, in general Congress assembled, appealing to the Supreme Judge of the world for the rectitude of our intentions, do, in the name, and by the authority of the good people of these colonies, solemnly publish and declare, that these united colonies are, and of right ought to be, free and independent states: that they are absolved from all allegiance to the British Crown, and that all political connection between them and the state of Great Britain is, and ought to be, totally dissolved; and that, as free and independent states, they have full power to levy war, conclude peace, contract alliances, establish commerce, and to do all other acts and things which independent states may of right do. And, for the support of this declaration, with a firm reliance on the protection of Divine Providence, we mutually pledge to each other our lives, our fortunes, and our sacred honor.

ARTICLES OF CONFEDERATION

Proposed by Congress November 15, 1777
Ratified and effective March 1, 1781

To all to whom these Presents shall come, we the undersigned Delegates of the States affixed to our Names send greeting.

Whereas the Delegates of the United States of America, in Congress assembled, did, on the fifteenth day of November in the Year of our Lord One Thousand Seven Hundred and Seventy seven, and in the Second Year of the Independence of America, agree to certain articles of Confederation and perpetual Union between the States of Newhampshire, Massachusetts-bay, Rhodeisland and Providence Plantations, Connecticut, New York, New Jersey, Pennsylvania, Delaware, Maryland, Virginia, North-Carolina, South-Carolina, and Georgia in the words followings, viz. "Articles of Confederation and perpetual Union between the states of Newhampshire, Massachusetts-bay, Rhodeisland and Providence Plantations, Connecticut, New-York, New-Jersey, Pennsylvania, Delaware, Maryland, Virginia, North-Carolina, South-Carolina and Georgia.

ARTICLE I.   The Stile of this Confederacy shall be "The United States of America."

ARTICLE II.   Each state retains its sovereignty, freedom, and independence, and every Power, Jurisdiction and right, which is not by this confederation expressly delegated to the United States, in Congress assembled.

ARTICLE III.   The said states hereby severally enter into a firm league of friendship with each other, for their common defence, the security of their Liberties, and their mutual and general welfare, binding themselves to assist each other, against all force offered to, or attacks made upon them, or any of them, on account of religion, sovereignty, trade, or any other pretence whatever.

ARTICLE IV. The better to secure and perpetuate mutual friendship and intercourse among the people of the different states in this union, the free inhabitants of each of these states, paupers, vagabonds and fugitives from justice excepted, shall be entitled to all privileges and immunities of free citizens in the several states; and the people of each state shall have free ingress and regress to and from any other state, and shall enjoy therein all the privileges of trade and commerce, subject to the same duties, impositions and restrictions as the inhabitants thereof respectively, provided that such restrictions shall not extend so far as to prevent the removal of property imported into any state, to any other state of which the Owner is an inhabitant; provided also that no imposition, duties or restrictions shall be laid by any state, on the property of the united states, or either of them.

If any Person guilty of, or charged with treason, felony, or other high misdeameanor in any state, shall flee from Justice, and be found in any of the united states, he shall, upon demand of the Governor or executive power, of the state from which he fled, be delivered up and removed to the state having jurisdiction of his offence.

Full faith and credit shall be given in each of these states to the records, acts and judicial proceedings of the courts and magistrates of every other state.

ARTICLE V. For the more convenient management of the general interests of the united states, delegates shall be annually appointed in such manner as the legislature of each state shall direct, to meet in Congress on the first Monday in November, in every year, with a power reserved to each state, to recall its delegates, or any of them, at any time within the year, and to send others in their stead, for the remainder of the Year.

No state shall be represented in Congress by less than two, nor by more than seven Members; and no person shall be capable of being a delegate for more than three years in any term of six years; nor shall any person, being a delegate, be capable of holding any office under the united states, for which he, or another of his benefit receives any salary, fees or emolument of any kind.

Each state shall maintain its own delegates in a meeting of the states, and while they act as members of the committee of the states.

In determining questions in the united states in Congress assembled, each state shall have one vote.

Freedom of speech and debate in Congress shall not be impeached or questioned in any Court, or place out of Congress, and the members of congress shall be protected in their persons from arrests and imprisonments, during the time of their going to and from, and attendance on Congress, except for treason, felony, or breach of the peace.

ARTICLE VI. No state without the Consent of the united states in congress assembled, shall send any embassy to, or receive any embassy from, or enter into any conference, agreement, alliance or treaty with any King, prince or state; nor shall any person holding any office of profit or trust under the united states, or any of them, accept of any present, emolument, office or title of any kind whatever from any king, prince or foreign state; nor shall the united states in congress assembled, or any of them, grant any title of nobility.

No two or more states shall enter into any treaty, confederation or alliance whatever between them, without the consent of the united states in congress assembled, specifying accurately the purposes for which the same is to be entered into, and how long it shall continue.

No state shall lay any imposts or duties, which may interfere with any stipulations in treaties, entered into by the United States in Congress assembled, with any king, prince or state, in pursuance of any treaties already proposed by congress, to the courts of France and Spain.

No vessels of war shall be kept up in time of peace by any state, except such number only, as shall be deemed necessary by the united states in congress assembled, for the defence of such state, or its trade; nor shall any body of forces be kept up by any state, in time of peace, except such number only, as in the judgment of the united states, in congress assembled, shall be deemed requisite

33

to garrison the forts necessary for the defence of such state; but every state shall always keep up a well regulated and disciplined militia, sufficiently armed and accoutred, and shall provide and constantly have ready for use, in public stores, a due number of field pieces and tents, and a proper quantity of arms, ammunition and camp equipage.

No state shall engage in any war without the consent of the united states in congress assembled, unless such state be actually invaded by enemies, or shall have received certain advice of a resolution being formed by some nation of Indians to invade such state, and the danger is so imminent as not to admit of a delay till the united states in congress assembled can be consulted: nor shall any state grant commissions to any ships or vessels of war, nor letters of marque or reprisal, except it be after a declaration of war by the united states in congress assembled, and then only against the kingdom or state and the subjects thereof, against which war has been so declared, and under such regulations as shall be established by the united states in congress assembled, unless such state be infested by pirates, in which case vessels of war may be fitted out for that occasion, and kept so long as the danger shall continue, or until the united states in congress assembled, shall determine otherwise.

ARTICLE VII. When land-forces are raised by any state for the common defence, all officers of or under the rank of colonel, shall be appointed by the legislature of each state respectively, by whom such forces shall be raised, or in such manner as such state shall direct, and all vacancies shall be filled up by the State which first made the appointment.

ARTICLE VIII. All charges of war, and all other expences that shall be incurred for the common defence or general welfare, and allowed by the united states in congress assembled, shall be defrayed out of a common treasury, which shall be supplied by the several states in proportion to the value of all land within each state, granted to or surveyed for any Person, as such land and the buildings and improvements thereon shall be estimated according to such mode as the united states in congress assembled, shall from time to time direct and appoint.

The taxes for paying that proportion shall be laid and levied by the authority and direction of the legislatures of the several states within the time agreed upon by the United States in Congress assembled.

ARTICLE IX. The united states in congress assembled, shall have the sole and exclusive right and power of determining on peace and war, except in the cases mentioned in the sixth article—of sending and receiving ambassadors—entering into treaties and alliances, provided that no treaty of commerce shall be made whereby the legislative power of the respective states shall be restrained from imposing such imposts and duties on foreigners as their own people are subjected to, or from prohibiting the exploration or importation of any species of goods or commodities, whatsoever—of establishing rules for deciding in all cases, what captures on land or water shall be legal, and in what manner prizes taken by land or naval forces in the service of the united states shall be divided or appropriated—of granting letters of marque and reprisal in times of peace—appointing courts for the trial of piracies and felonies commited on the high seas and establishing courts for receiving and determining finally appeals in all cases of captures, provided that no member of congress shall be appointed a judge of any of the said courts.

The united states in congress assembled shall also be the last resort on appeal in all disputes and differences now subsisting or that hereafter may arise between two or more states concerning boundary, jurisdiction or any other cause whatever; which authority shall always be exercised in the manner following. Whenever the legislative or executive authority or lawful agent of any state in controversy with another shall present a petition to congress stating the matter in question and praying for a hearing, notice thereof shall be given by order of congress to the legislative or executive authority of the other state in controversy, and a day assigned for the appearance of the parties by their lawful agents, who shall then be directed to appoint by joint consent, commissioners or judges to constitute a court for hearing and determining the matter in question: but if they cannot agree, congress shall name three persons out of each of the united states, and from the list of such persons each party shall alternately strike out one, the petitioners beginning, until the number shall be reduced to thirteen; and from that number not less than seven, nor more than nine names as congress shall direct, shall in the presence of congress be drawn out by lot, and the persons whose names shall be so drawn or any five of them, shall be commissioners or judges, to hear and finally determine the controversy, so always as a major part of the judges who shall hear the cause shall agree in the determination: and if either party shall neglect to attend at the day appointed, without showing reasons, which congress shall judge sufficient, or being present shall refuse to strike, the congress shall proceed to nominate three persons out of each state, and the secretary of congress shall strike in behalf of such party absent or refusing; and the judgment and sentence of the court to be appointed, in the manner before prescribed, shall be final and conclusive; and if any of the parties shall refuse to submit to the authority of such court, or to appear or defend their claim or cause, the court shall nevertheless proceed to pronounce sentence, or judgment, which shall in like manner be final and decisive, the judgment or sentence and other proceedings being in either case transmitted to congress, and lodged among the acts of congress for the security of the parties concerned: provided that every commissioner, before he sits in judgment, shall take an oath to be administered by one of the judges of the supreme or superior court of the state where the cause shall be tried, "well and truly to hear and determine the matter in question, according to the best of his judgment, without favour, affection or hope of reward:" provided also, that no state shall be deprived of territory for the benefit of the united states.

All controversies concerning the private right of soil claimed under different grants of two or more states, whose jurisdictions as they may respect such lands, and the states which passed such grants are adjusted, the said grants or either of them being at the same time claimed to have originated antecedent to such settlement of jurisdiction, shall on the petition of either party to the congress of the united states, be finally determined as near as may be in the same manner as is before prescribed for deciding disputes respecting territorial jurisdiction between different states.

The united states in congress assembled shall also have the sole and exclusive right and power of regulating the alloy and value of coin struck by their own authority, or by that of the respective states—fixing the standard of weights and measures throughout the united states—regulating the trade and managing all affairs with the Indians, not members of any of the states, provided that the legislative right of any state within its own limits be not infringed or violated—establishing and regulating post-offices from one state to another, throughout all the united states, and exacting such postage on the papers passing thro' the same as may be requisite to defray the expences of the said office—appointing all officers of the land forces, in the service of the united states, excepting regimental officers—appointing all the officers of the naval forces, and commissioning all officers whatever in the service of the united states—making rules for the government and regulation of the said land and naval forces, and directing their operations.

The united states in congress assembled shall have authority to appoint a committee, to sit in the recess of congress, to be denominated "A Committee of the States," and to consist of one delegate from each state; and to appoint such other committees and civil officers as may be necessary for managing the general affairs of the united states under their direction—to appoint one of their number to preside, provided that no person be allowed to serve in the office of president more than one year in any term of three years; to ascertain the necessary sums of money to be raised for the service of the united states, and to appropriate and apply the same for defraying the public expences—to borrow money, or emit bills on the credit of the united states, transmitting every half year to the respective states on account of the sums of money so borrowed or emitted,—to build and equip a navy—to agree upon the number of land forces, and to make requisitions from each state for its quota, in proportion to the number of white inhabitants in such state; which requisition shall be binding, and thereupon the legislature of each state shall appoint the regimental officers, raise the men and cloath, arm and equip them in a soldier like manner, at the expence of the united states; and the officers and men so cloathed, armed and equipped shall march to the place appointed, and within the time agreed on by the united states in congress assembled: But if the united states in congress assembled shall, on consideration of circumstances judge proper that any state should not raise men, or should raise a smaller number than its quota, and that any other state should raise a greater number of men than the quota thereof, such extra number shall be raised, officered, cloathed, armed and equipped in the same manner as the quota of such state, unless the legislature of such state shall judge that such extra number cannot be safely spared out of the same, in which case they shall raise officer, cloath, arm and equip as many of such extra number as they judge can be safely spared. And the officers and men so cloathed, armed and equipped, shall march to the place appointed, and within the time agreed on by the united states in congress assembled.

The united states in congress assembled shall never engage in a war, nor grant letters or marque and reprisal in time of peace, nor enter into any treaties or alliances, nor coin money, nor regulate the value thereof, nor ascertain the sums and expences necessary for the defence and welfare of the united states, or any of them, nor emit bills, nor borrow money on the credit of the united states, nor appropriate money, nor agree upon the number of vessels of war, to be built or purchased, or the number of land or sea forces to be raised, nor appoint a commander in chief of the army or navy, unless nine states assent to the same: nor shall a question on any other point, except for adjourning from day to day be determined, unless by the votes of a majority of the united states in congress assembled.

The congress of the united states shall have power to adjourn to any time within the year, and to any place within the united states, so that no period of adjournment be for a longer duration than the space of six Months, and shall publish the Journal of their proceedings monthly, except such parts thereof relating to treaties, alliances or military operations, as in their judgment require secrecy; and the yeas and nays of the delegates of each state on any question shall be entered on the Journal, when it is desired by any delegate; and the delegates of a state, or any of them, at his or their request shall be furnished with a transcript of the said Journal, except such parts as are above excepted, to lay before the legislatures of the several states.

ARTICLE X.   The committee of the states, or any nine of them, shall be authorized to execute, in the recess of congress, such of the powers of congress as the united states in congress assembled, by the consent of nine states, shall from time to time think expedient to vest them with; provided that no power be delegated to the said committee, for the exercise of which, by the articles of confederation, the voice of nine states in the congress of the united states assembled is requisite.

ARTICLE XI.   Canada acceding to this confederation, and joining in the measures of the united states, shall be admitted into, and entitled to all the advantages of this union: but no other colony shall be admitted into the same, unless such admission be agreed to by nine states.

ARTICLE XII.   All bills of credit emitted, monies borrowed and debts contracted by, or under the authority of Congress, before the assembling of the united states, in pursuance of the present confederation, shall be deemed and considered as a charge against the united states, for payment and satisfaction whereof the said united states, and the public faith are hereby solemnly pledged.

ARTICLE XIII.   Every state shall abide by the determinations of the united states in congress assembled, on all questions which by this confederation are submitted to them. And the Articles of this confederation shall be inviolably observed by every state, and the union shall be perpetual; nor shall any alteration at any time hereafter be made in any of them; unless such alteration be agreed to in a congress of the united states, and be afterwards confirmed by the legislatures of every state.

And Whereas it has pleased the Great Governor of the World to incline the hearts of the legislatures we respectively represent in congress, to approve of, and to authorize us to ratify the said articles of confederation and perpetual union. Know Ye that we the undersigned delegates, by virtue of the power and authority to us given for that purpose, do by these presents, in the name and in behalf of our respective constituents, fully and entirely ratify and confirm each and every of the said articles of confederation and perpetual union, and all and singular the matters and things therein contained: And we do further solemnly plight and engage the faith of our respective constituents, that they shall abide by the determinations of the united states in congress assembled, on all questions, which by the said confederation are submitted to them. And that the articles thereof shall be inviolably observed by the states we respectively represent, and that the union shall be perpetual. In Witness whereof we have hereunto set our hands in Congress. Done at Philadelphia in the state of Pennsylvania the ninth day of July, in the year of our Lord one Thousand seven Hundred and Seventy-eight, and in the third year of the independence of America. [Names omitted]

CONSTITUTION
OF THE UNITED STATES

Proposed by Convention September 17, 1787
Effective March 4, 1789

WE the people of the United States, in order to form a more perfect union, establish justice, insure domestic tranquillity, provide for the common defense, promote the general welfare, and secure the blessings of liberty to ourselves and our posterity, do ordain and establish this Constitution for the United States of America.

ARTICLE I

SECTION 1.   All legislative powers herein granted shall be vested in a Congress of the United States, which shall consist of a Senate and House of Representatives.

SECTION 2.   1.   The House of Representatives shall be composed of members chosen every second year by the people of the several States, and the electors in each State shall have the qualifications requisite for electors of the most numerous branch of the State legislature.

2.   No person shall be a representative who shall not have attained to the age of twenty-five years, and been seven years a citizen of the United States, and who shall not, when elected, be an inhabitant of that State in which he shall be chosen.

3.   Representatives [and direct taxes]* shall be apportioned among the several States which may be included within this Union, according to their respective numbers, [which shall be determined

*See the Sixteenth Amendment.

41

by adding to the whole number of free persons, including those bound to service for a term of years, and excluding Indians not taxed, three fifths of all other persons.]* The actual enumeration shall be made within three years after the first meeting of the Congress of the United States, and within every subsequent term of ten years, in such manner as they shall by law direct. The number of representatives shall not exceed one for every thirty thousand, but each State shall have at least one representative; and until such enumeration shall be made, the State of New Hampshire shall be entitled to choose three, Massachusetts eight, Rhode Island and Providence Plantations one, Connecticut five, New York six, New Jersey four, Pennsylvania eight, Delaware one, Maryland six, Virginia ten, North Carolina five, South Carolina five, and Georgia three.

4. When vacancies happen in the representation from any State, the executive authority thereof shall issue writs of election to fill such vacancies.

5. The House of Representatives shall choose their speaker and other officers; and shall have the sole power of impeachment.

SECTION 3. 1. The Senate of the United States shall be composed of two senators from each State, [chosen by the legislature thereof,]† for six years; and each senator shall have one vote.

2. Immediately after they shall be assembled in consequence of the first election, they shall be divided as equally as may be into three classes. The seats of the senators of the first class shall be vacated at the expiration of the second year, of the second class at the expiration of the fourth year, and of the third class at the expiration of the sixth year, so that one third may be chosen every second year; and if vacancies happen by resignation, or otherwise, during the recess of the legislature of any State, the executive thereof may make temporary appointments until the next meeting of the legislature, which shall then fill such vacancies.†

3. No person shall be a senator who shall not have attained to

*See the Fourteenth Amendment.
†See the Seventeenth Amendment.

the age of thirty years, and been nine years a citizen of the United States, and who shall not, when elected, be an inhabitant of that State for which he shall be chosen.

4.   The Vice President of the United States shall be President of the Senate, but shall nave no vote, unless they be equally divided.

5.   The Senate shall choose their other officers, and also a president *pro tempore,* in the absence of the Vice President, or when he shall exercise the office of the President of the United States.

6.   The Senate shall have the sole power to try all impeachments. When sitting for that purpose, they shall be on oath or affirmation. When the President of the United States is tried, the chief justice shall preside: and no person shall be convicted without the concurrence of two thirds of the members present.

7.   Judgment in cases of impeachment shall not extend further than to removal from office, and disqualifications to hold and enjoy any office of honor, trust or profit under the United States: but the party convicted shall nevertheless be liable and subject to indictment, trial, judgment and punishment, according to law.

SECTION 4.   1.   The times, places, and manner of holding elections for senators and representatives, shall be prescribed in each State by the legislature thereof; but the Congress may at any time by law make or alter such regulations, except as to the places of choosing senators.

2.   The Congress shall assemble at least once in every year, and such meeting shall be on [the first Monday in December, unless they shall by law appoint a different day.]*

SECTION 5.   1.   Each House shall be the judge of the elections, returns and qualifications of its own members, and a majority of each shall constitute a quorum to do business; but a smaller number may adjourn from day to day, and may be authorized to compel the attendance of absent members, in such manner, and under such penalties as each House may provide.

2.   Each House may determine the rules of its proceedings,

*See the Twentieth Amendment.

punish its members for disorderly behavior, and, with the concurrence of two thirds, expel a member.

3. Each House shall keep a journal of its proceedings, and from time to time publish the same, excepting such parts as may in their judgment require secrecy; and the yeas and nays of the members of either House on any question shall, at the desire of one fifth of those present, be entered on the journal.

4. Neither House, during the session of Congress, shall, without the consent of the other, adjourn for more than three days, nor to any other place than that in which the two Houses shall be sitting.

SECTION 6. 1. The senators and representatives shall receive a compensation for their services, to be ascertained by law, and paid out of the Treasury of the United States. They shall in all cases, except treason, felony, and breach of the peace, be privileged from arrest during their attendance at the session of their respective Houses, and in going to and returning from the same; and for any speech or debate in either House, they shall not be questioned in any other place.

2. No senator or representative shall, during the time for which he was elected, be appointed to any civil office under the authority of the United States, which shall have been created, or the emoluments whereof shall have been increased during such time; and no person holding any office under the United States shall be a member of either House during his continuance in office.

SECTION 7. 1. All bills for raising revenue shall originate in the House of Representatives; but the Senate may propose or concur with amendments as on other bills.

2. Every bill which shall have passed the House of Representatives and the Senate, shall, before it becomes a law, be presented to the President of the United States; if he approves he shall sign it, but if not he shall return it, with his objections to that House in which it shall have originated, who shall enter the objections at large on their journal, and proceed to reconsider it. If after such reconsideration two thirds of that House shall agree to pass the bill, it shall be sent, together with the objections, to the

other House, by which it shall likewise be reconsidered, and if approved by two thirds of that House, it shall become a law. But in all such cases the votes of both Houses shall be determined by yeas and nays, and the names of the persons voting for and against the bill shall be entered on the journal of each House respectively. If any bill shall not be returned by the President within ten days (Sundays excepted) after it shall have been presented to him, the same shall be a law, in like manner as if he had signed it, unless the Congress by their adjournment prevent its return, in which case it shall not be a law.

3.   Every order, resolution, or vote to which the concurrence of the Senate and the House of Representatives may be necessary (except on a question of adjournment) shall be presented to the President of the United States; and before the same shall take effect, shall be approved by him, or being disapproved by him, shall be repassed by two thirds of the Senate and House of Representatives, according to the rules and limitations prescribed in the case of a bill.

SECTION 8.   The Congress shall have the power

1.   To lay and collect taxes, duties, imposts, and excises, to pay the debts and provide for the common defense and general welfare of the United States; but all duties, imposts, and excises shall be uniform throughout the United States;

2.   To borrow money on the credit of the United States;

3.   To regulate commerce with foreign nations, and among the several States, and with the Indian tribes;

4.   To establish a uniform rule of naturalization, and uniform laws on the subject of bankruptcies throughout the United States;

5.   To coin money, regulate the value thereof, and of foreign coin, and fix the standard of weights and measures;

6.   To provide for the punishment of counterfeiting the securities and current coin of the United States;

7.   To establish post offices and post roads:

8.   To promote the progress of science and useful arts, by securing for limited times to authors and inventors the exclusive right to their respective writings and discoveries;

9. To constitute tribunals inferior to the Supreme Court;

10. To define and punish piracies and felonies committed on the high seas, and offenses against the law of nations;

11. To declare war, grant letters of marque and reprisal, and make rules concerning captures on land and water;

12. To raise and support armies, but no appropriation of money to that use shall be for a longer term than two years;

13. To provide and maintain a navy;

14. To make rules for the government and regulation of the land and naval forces;

15. To provide for calling forth the militia to execute the laws of the Union, suppress insurrections and repel invasions;

16. To provide for organizing, arming, and disciplining the militia, and for governing such part of them as may be employed in the service of the United States, reserving to the States respectively, the appointment of the officers, and the authority of training the militia according to the discipline prescribed by Congress;

17. To exercise exclusive legislation in all cases whatsoever, over such district (not exceeding ten miles square) as may, by cession of particular States, and the acceptance of Congress, become the seat of the government of the United States, and to exercise like authority over all places purchased by the consent of the legislature of the State in which the same shall be, for the erection of forts, magazines, arsenals, dockyards, and other needful buildings; and

18. To make all laws which shall be necessary and proper for carrying into execution the foregoing powers, and all other powers vested by this Constitution in the government of the United States, or in any department or officer thereof.

SECTION 9. 1. The migration or importation of such persons as any of the States now existing shall think proper to admit, shall not be prohibited by the Congress prior to the year one thousand eight hundred and eight, but a tax or duty may be imposed on such importation, not exceeding ten dollars for each person.

2. The privilege of the writ of *habeas corpus* shall not be sus-

pended, unless when in cases of rebellion or invasion the public safety may require it.

3. No bill of attainder or *ex post facto* law shall be passed.

4. No capitation, or other direct, tax shall be laid unless in proportion to the census or enumeration hereinbefore directed to be taken.*

5. No tax or duty shall be laid on articles exported from any State.

6. No preference shall be given by any regulation of commerce or revenue to the ports of one State over those of another: nor shall vessels bound to, or from, one State be obliged to enter, clear, or pay duties in another.

7. No money shall be drawn from the treasury, but in consequence of appropriations made by law; and a regular statement and account of the receipts and expenditures of all public money shall be published from time to time.

8. No title of nobility shall be granted by the United States: and no person holding any office of profit or trust under them, shall, without the consent of the Congress, accept of any present, emolument, office, or title, of any kind whatever, from any king, prince, or foreign State.

SECTION 10. 1. No State shall enter into any treaty, alliance, or confederation; grant letters of marque and reprisal; coin money; emit bills of credit; make anything but gold and silver coin a tender in payment of debts; pass any bill of attainder, *ex post facto* law, or law impairing the obligation of contracts, or grant any title of nobility.

2. No State shall, without the consent of the Congress, lay any imposts or duties on imports or exports, except what may be absolutely necessary for executing its inspection laws; and the net produce of all duties and imposts laid by any State on imports or exports, shall be for the use of the treasury of the United States; and all such laws shall be subject to the revision and control of the Congress.

*See the Sixteenth Amendment.

3.   No State shall, without the consent of the Congress, lay any duty of tonnage, keep troops, or ships of war in time of peace, enter into any agreement or compact with another State, or with a foreign power, or engage in war, unless actually invaded, or in such imminent danger as will not admit of delay.

ARTICLE II

SECTION 1.   1.   The executive power shall be vested in a President of the United States of America. He shall hold his office during the term of four years, and, together with the Vice President, chosen for the same term, be elected as follows:

2.   Each State* shall appoint, in such manner as the legislature thereof may direct, a number of electors, equal to the whole number of senators and representatives to which the State may be entitled in the Congress: but no senator or representative, or person holding an office of trust or profit under the United States, shall be appointed an elector.

3.   The electors shall meet in their respective States, and vote by ballot for two persons, of whom one at least shall not be an inhabitant of the same State with themselves. And they shall make a list of all the persons voted for, and of the number of votes for each; which list they shall sign and certify, and transmit sealed to the seat of the government of the United States, directed to the president of the Senate. The president of the Senate shall, in the presence of the Senate and House of Representatives, open all the certificates, and the votes shall then be counted. The person having the greatest number of votes shall be the President, if such number be a majority of the whole number of electors appointed; and if there be more than one who have such majority, and have an equal number of votes, then the House of Representatives shall immediately choose by ballot one of them for President; and if no person have a majority, then from the five highest on the list the said House shall in like manner choose the President. But in choos-

*See the Twenty-third Amendment.

ing the President, the votes shall be taken by States, the representation from each State having one vote; a quorum for this purpose shall consist of a member or members from two thirds of the States, and a majority of all the States shall be necessary to a choice. In every case, after the choice of the President, the person having the greatest number of votes of the electors shall be the Vice President. But if there should remain two or more who have equal votes, the Senate shall choose from them by ballot the Vice President.*

4.   The Congress may determine the time of choosing the electors, and the day on which they shall give their votes; which day shall be the same throughout the United States.

5.   No person except a natural born citizen, or a citizen of the United States, at the time of the adoption of this Constitution, shall be eligible to the office of President; neither shall any person be eligible to that office who shall not have attained to the age of thirty-five years, and been fourteen years a resident within the United States.

6.   In case of the removal of the President from office, or of his death, resignation, or inability to discharge the powers and duties of the said office, the same shall devolve on the Vice President, and the Congress may by law provide for the case of removal, death, resignation, or inability, both of the President and Vice President, declaring what officer shall then act as President, and such officer shall act accordingly, until the disability be removed, or a President shall be elected.†

7.   The President shall, at stated times, receive for his services a compensation, which shall neither be increased nor diminished during the period for which he shall have been elected, and he shall not receive within that period any other emolument from the United States, or any of them.

8.   Before he enter on the execution of his office, he shall take the following oath or affirmation:—"I do solemnly swear (or affirm) that I will faithfully execute the office of President of the

---

*The Twelfth Amendment supersedes this paragraph.
†See the Twenty-fifth Amendment.

United States, and will to the best of my ability, preserve, protect and defend the Constitution of the United States."

SECTION 2. 1. The President shall be commander in chief of the army and navy of the United States, and of the militia of the several States, when called into the actual service of the United States; he may require the opinion, in writing, of the principal officer in each of the executive departments, upon any subject relating to the duties of their respective offices, and he shall have power to grant reprieves and pardons for offenses against the United States, except in cases of impeachment.

2. He shall have power, by and with the advice and consent of the Senate, to make treaties, provided two thirds of the senators present concur; and he shall nominate, and by and with the advice and consent of the Senate, shall appoint ambassadors, other public ministers and consuls, judges of the Supreme Court, and all other officers of the United States, whose appointments are not herein otherwise provided for, and which shall be established by law: but the Congress may by law vest the appointment of such inferior officers, as they think proper, in the President alone, in the courts of law, or in the heads of departments.

3. The President shall have power to fill up all vacancies that may happen during the recess of the Senate, by granting commissions which shall expire at the end of their next session.

SECTION 3. He shall from time to time give to the Congress information of the state of the Union, and recommend to their consideration such measures as he shall judge necessary and expedient; he may, on extraordinary occasions, convene both Houses, or either of them, and in case of disagreement between them with respect to the time of adjournment, he may adjourn them to such time as he shall think proper; he shall receive ambassadors and other public ministers; he shall take care that the laws be faithfully executed, and shall commission all the officers of the United States.

SECTION 4. The President, Vice President, and all civil officers of the United States, shall be removed from office on impeachment for and conviction of, treason, bribery, or other high crimes and misdemeanors.

Article III

section 1.   The judicial power of the United States shall be vested in one Supreme Court, and in such inferior courts as the Congress may from time to time ordain and establish. The judges, both of the Supreme and inferior courts, shall hold their offices during good behavior, and shall, at stated times, receive for their services, a compensation, which shall not be diminished during their continuance in office.

section 2.   1.   The judicial power shall extend to all cases, in law and equity, arising under this Constitution, the laws of the United States, and treaties made, or which shall be made, under their authority;—to all cases affecting ambassadors, other public ministers and consuls;—to all cases of admiralty and maritime jurisdiction;—to controversies to which the United States shall be a party;—to controversies between two or more States;—between a State and citizens of another State;*—between citizens of different States;—between citizens of the same State claiming lands under grants of different States, and between a State, or the citizens thereof, and foreign States, citizens or subjects.

2.   In all cases affecting ambassadors, other public ministers and consuls, and those in which a State shall be party, the Supreme Court shall have original jurisdiction. In all the other cases before mentioned, the Supreme Court shall have appellate jurisdiction, both as to law and to fact, with such exceptions, and under such regulations as the Congress shall make.

3.   The trial of all crimes, except in cases of impeachment, shall be by jury; and such trial shall be held in the State where the said crimes shall have been committed; but when not committed within any State, the trial shall be at such place or places as the Congress may by law have directed.

section 3.   1.   Treason against the United States shall consist only in levying war against them, or in adhering to their enemies, giving them aid and comfort. No person shall be convicted of

*See the Eleventh Amendment.

51

treason unless on the testimony of two witnesses to the same overt act, or on confession in open court.

2. The Congress shall have power to declare the punishment of treason, but no attainder of treason shall work corruption of blood, or forfeiture except during the life of the person attained.

ARTICLE IV

SECTION 1. Full faith and credit shall be given in each State to the public acts, records, and judicial proceedings of every other State. And the Congress may by general laws prescribe the manner in which such acts, records and proceedings shall be proved, and the effect thereof.

SECTION 2. 1. The citizens of each State shall be entitled to all privileges and immunities of citizens in the several States.

2. A person charged in any State with treason, felony, or other crime, who shall flee from justice, and be found in another State, shall on demand of the executive authority of the State from which he fled, be delivered up to be removed to the State having jurisdiction of the crime.

3. No person held to service or labor in one State under the laws thereof, escaping into another, shall, in consequence of any law or regulation therein, be discharged from such service or labor, but shall be delivered up on claim of the party to whom such service or labor may be due.*

SECTION 3. 1. New States may be admitted by the Congress into this Union; but no new State shall be formed or erected within the jurisdiction of any other State; nor any State be formed by the junction of two or more States, or parts of States, without the consent of the legislatures of the States concerned as well as of Congress.

2. The Congress shall have power to dispose of and make all needful rules and regulations respecting the territory or other property belonging to the United States; and nothing in this Consti-

*See the Thirteenth Amendment.

tution shall be so construed as to prejudice any claims of the United States, or of any particular State.

SECTION 4.   The United States shall guarantee to every State in this Union a republican form of government, and shall protect each of them against invasion; and on application of the legislature, or of the executive (when the legislature cannot be convened) against domestic violence.

ARTICLE V

The Congress, whenever two thirds of both Houses shall deem it necessary, shall propose amendments to this Constitution, or, on the application of the legislatures of two thirds of the several States, shall call a convention for proposing amendments, which in either case, shall be valid to all intents and purposes, as part of this Constitution when ratified by the legislatures of three fourths of the several States, or by conventions in three fourths thereof, as the one or the other mode of ratification may be proposed by the Congress; Provided that no amendment which may be made prior to the year one thousand eight hundred and eight shall in any manner affect the first and fourth clauses in the ninth section of the first article; and that no State, without its consent, shall be deprived of its equal suffrage in the Senate.

ARTICLE VI

1.   All debts contracted and engagements entered into, before the adoption of this Constitution, shall be as valid against the United States under this Constitution, as under the Confederation.

2.   This Constitution, and the laws of the United States which shall be made in pursuance thereof; and all treaties made, or which shall be made, under the authority of the United States, shall be the supreme law of the land; and the Judges in every State shall be bound thereby, anything in the Constitution or laws of any State to the contrary notwithstanding.

3.   The senators and representatives before mentioned, and the

members of the several State legislatures, and all executive and judicial officers, both of the United States and of the several States, shall be bound by oath or affirmation to support this Constitution; but no religious test shall ever be required as a qualification to any office or public trust under the United States.

ARTICLE VII

The ratification of the conventions of nine States shall be sufficient for the establishment of this Constitution between the States so ratifying the same.

Done in Convention by the unanimous consent of the States present the seventeenth day of September in the year of our Lord one thousand seven hundred and eighty-seven, and of the independence of the United States of America the twelfth. In witness whereof we have hereunto subscribed our names. [Names omitted]

Articles in addition to, and amendment of, the Constitution of the United States of America, proposed by Congress, and ratified by the legislatures of the several States pursuant to the fifth article of the original Constitution.

AMENDMENTS

First Ten Amendments passed by Congress Sept. 25, 1789. Ratified by three-fourths of the States December 15, 1791.

AMENDMENT I

Congress shall make no law respecting an establishment of religion, or prohibiting the free exercise thereof; or abridging the freedom of speech, or of the press; or the right of the people peaceably to assemble, and to petition the government for a redress of grievances.

AMENDMENT II

A well regulated militia, being necessary to the security of a free State, the right of the people to keep and bear arms, shall not be infringed.

AMENDMENT III

No soldier shall, in time of peace be quartered in any house, without the consent of the owner, nor in time of war, but in a manner to be prescribed by law.

AMENDMENT IV

The right of the people to be secure in their persons, houses, papers, and effects, against unreasonable searches and seizures, shall not be violated, and no warrants shall issue, but upon probable cause, supported by oath or affirmation, and particularly describing the place to be searched, and the persons or things to be seized.

AMENDMENT V

No person shall be held to answer for a capital, or otherwise infamous crime, unless on a presentment or indictment of a grand jury, except in cases arising in the land or naval forces, or in the militia, when in actual service in time of war or public danger; nor shall any person be subject for the same offense to be twice put in jeopardy of life or limb; nor shall be compelled in any criminal case to be a witness against himself, nor be deprived of life, liberty, or property, without due process of law; nor shall private property be taken for public use without just compensation.

AMENDMENT VI

In all criminal prosecutions, the accused shall enjoy the right to a speedy and public trial, by an impartial jury of the State and district wherein the crime shall have been committed, which district shall have been previously ascertained by law, and to be informed of the nature and cause of the accusation; to be confronted with the witnesses against him; to have compulsory process for obtaining witnesses in his favor, and to have the assistance of counsel for his defense.

Amendment VII

In suits at common law, where the value in controversy shall exceed twenty dollars, the right of trial by jury shall be preserved, and no fact tried by a jury shall be otherwise re-examined in any court of the United States, than according to the rules of the common law.

Amendment VIII

Excessive bail shall not be required, nor excessive fines imposed, nor cruel and unusual punishments inflicted.

Amendment IX

The enumeration in the Constitution of certain rights shall not be construed to deny or disparage others retained by the people.

Amendment X

The powers not delegated to the United States by the Constitution, nor prohibited by it to the States, are reserved to the States respectively, or to the people.

Amendment XI

Passed by Congress March 4, 1794. Ratified February 7, 1798.

The judicial power of the United States shall not be construed to extend to any suit in law or equity, commenced or prosecuted against one of the United States by citizens of another State, or by citizens or subjects of any foreign State.

Amendment XII

Passed by Congress December 9, 1803. Ratified July 27, 1804.

The electors shall meet in their respective States, and vote by ballot for President and Vice President, one of whom, at least, shall not be an inhabitant of the same State with themselves; they shall name in their ballots the person voted for as President, and in distinct ballots, the person voted for as Vice President, and they shall make distinct lists of all persons voted for as President and of all persons voted for as Vice President, and of the number of votes for each, which lists they shall sign and certify, and transmit sealed to the seat of the government of the United States, directed to the President of the Senate;—The President of the Senate shall, in the presence of the Senate and House of Representatives, open all the certificates and the votes shall then be counted;—The person having the greatest number of votes for President, shall be the President, if such number be a majority of the whole number of electors appointed; and if no person have such majority, then from the persons having the highest numbers not exceeding three on the list of those voted for as President, the House of Representatives shall choose immediately, by ballot, the President. But in choosing the President, the votes shall be taken by States, the representation from each State having one vote; a quorum for this purpose shall consist of a member or members from two thirds of the States, and a majority of all the States shall be necessary to a choice. And if the House of Representatives shall not choose a President whenever the right of choice shall devolve upon them, before the fourth day of March next following, then the Vice President shall act as President, as in the case of the death or other constitutional disability of the President. The person having the greatest number of votes as Vice President shall be the Vice President, if such number be a majority of the whole number of electors appointed, and if no person have a majority, then from the two highest numbers on the list, the Senate shall choose the Vice President; a quorum for the purpose shall consist of two thirds of the whole number of Senators, and a majority of the whole number shall be necessary to a choice. But no person constitutionally ineligible to the office of President shall be eligible to that of Vice President of the United States.

Amendment XIII

Passed by Congress January 31, 1865. Ratified December 6, 1865.

SECTION 1.   Neither slavery nor involuntary servitude, except as punishment for crime whereof the party shall have been duly convicted, shall exist within the United States, or any place subject to their jurisdiction.

SECTION 2.   Congress shall have power to enforce this article by appropriate legislation.

Amendment XIV

Passed by Congress June 13, 1866. Ratified July 9, 1868.

SECTION 1.   All persons born or naturalized in the United States, and subject to the jurisdiction thereof, are citizens of the United States and of the State wherein they reside. No State shall make or enforce any law which shall abridge the privileges or immunities of citizens of the United States; nor shall any State deprive any person of life, liberty, or property, without due process of law; nor deny to any person within its jurisdiction the equal protection of the laws.

SECTION 2.   Representatives shall be apportioned among the several States according to their respective numbers, counting the whole number of persons in each State, excluding Indians not taxed. But when the right to vote at any election for the choice of electors for President and Vice President of the United States, representatives in Congress, the executive and judicial officers of a State, or the members of the legislature thereof, is denied to any of the male inhabitants of such State, being twenty-one years of age, and citizens of the United States, or in any way abridged, except for participation in rebellion, or other crime, the basis of representation therein shall be reduced in the proportion which the number of such male citizens shall bear to the whole number of male citizens twenty-one years of age in such State.

SECTION 3. No person shall be a senator or representative in Congress, or elector of President and Vice President, or hold any office, civil or military, under the United States, or under any State, who having previously taken an oath, as a member of Congress, or as an officer of the United States, or as a member of any State legislature, or as an executive or judicial officer of any State, to support the Constitution of the United States, shall have engaged in insurrection or rebellion against the same, or given aid or comfort to the enemies thereof. But Congress may by a vote of two thirds of each House, remove such disability.

SECTION 4. The validity of the public debt of the United States, authorized by law, including debts incurred for payment of pensions and bounties for services in suppressing insurrection or rebellion, shall not be questioned. But neither the United States nor any State shall assume or pay any debt or obligation incurred in aid of insurrection or rebellion against the United States, or any claim for the loss or emancipation of any slave; but all such debts, obligations, and claims shall be held illegal and void.

SECTION 5. The Congress shall have power to enforce, by appropriate legislation, the provisions of this article.

Amendment XV

Passed by Congress February 26, 1869. Ratified February 3, 1870.

SECTION 1. The right of citizens of the United States to vote shall not be denied or abridged by the United States or by any State on account of race, color, or previous condition of servitude.

SECTION 2.   The Congress shall have power to enforce this article by appropriate legislation.

AMENDMENT XVI

Passed by Congress July 2, 1909. Ratified February 3, 1913.

The Congress shall have power to lay and collect taxes on incomes, from whatever source derived, without apportionment among the several States, and without regard to any census or enumeration.

AMENDMENT XVII

Passed by Congress May 13, 1912. Ratified April 8, 1913.

The Senate of the United States shall be composed of two senators from each state, elected by the people thereof, for six years; and each senator shall have one vote. The electors in each State shall have the qualifications requisite for electors of the most numerous branch of the State legislature.

When vacancies happen in the representation of any State in the Senate, the executive authority of such State shall issue writs of election to fill such vacancies: *Provided,* That the legislature of any State may empower the executive thereof to make temporary appointments until the people fill the vacancies by election as the legislature may direct.

This amendment shall not be so construed as to affect the election or term of any senator chosen before it becomes valid as part of the Constitution.

Amendment XVIII*

Passed by Congress December 18, 1917. Ratified January 16, 1919.

After one year from the ratification of this article, the manufacture, sale, or transportation of intoxicating liquors within, the importation thereof into, or the exportation thereof from the United States and all territory subject to the jurisdiction thereof for beverage purposes is hereby prohibited.

The Congress and the several States shall have concurrent power to enforce this article by appropriate legislation.

This article shall be inoperative unless it shall have been ratified as an amendment to the Constitution by the legislatures of the several States, as provided in the Constitution, within seven years from the date of the submission hereof to the states by Congress.

Amendment XIX

Passed by Congress June 4, 1919. Ratified August 18, 1920.

The right of citizens of the United States to vote shall not be denied or abridged by the United States or by any State on account of sex.

The Congress shall have power by appropriate legislation to enforce the provisions of this article.

Amendment XX

Passed by Congress March 2, 1932. Ratified January 23, 1933.

SECTION 1.   The terms of the President and Vice President shall end at noon on the 20th day of January, and the terms of Senators

---

*Repealed by the Twenty-first Amendment.

and Representatives at noon on the 3d day of January, of the years in which such terms would have ended if this article had not been ratified; and the terms of their successors shall then begin.

SECTION 2.   The Congress shall assemble at least once in every year, and such meeting shall begin at noon on the 3d day of January, unless they shall by law appoint a different day.

SECTION 3.   If, at the time fixed for the beginning of the term of the President, the President-elect shall have died, the Vice President-elect shall become President. If a President shall not have been chosen before the time fixed for the beginning of his term, or if the President-elect shall have failed to qualify, then the Vice President-elect shall act as President until a President shall have qualified; and the Congress may by law provide for the case wherein neither a President-elect nor a Vice President-elect shall have qualified, declaring who shall then act as President, or the manner in which one who is to act shall be selected, and such person shall act accordingly until a President or Vice President shall have qualified.

SECTION 4.   The Congress may by law provide for the case of the death of any of the persons from whom the House of Representatives may choose a President whenever the right of choice shall have devolved upon them, and for the case of the death of any of the persons from whom the Senate may choose a Vice President whenever the right of choice shall have devolved upon them.

SECTION 5.   Sections 1 and 2 shall take effect on the 15th day of October following the ratification of this article.

SECTION 6.   This article shall be inoperative unless it shall have been ratified as an amendment to the Constitution by the legislatures of three-fourths of the several States within seven years from the date of its submission.

Amendment XXI

Passed by Congress February 20, 1933. Ratified December 5, 1933.

SECTION 1.   The Eighteenth Article of amendment to the Constitution of the United States is hereby repealed.

SECTION 2.   The transportation or importation into any State, Territory, or possession of the United States for delivery or use therein of intoxicating liquors in violation of the laws thereof, is hereby prohibited.

SECTION 3.   This article shall be inoperative unless it shall have been ratified as an amendment to the Constitution by conventions in the several States, as provided in the Constitution, within seven years from the date of the submission thereof to the States by the Congress.

AMENDMENT XXII

Passed by Congress March 21, 1947. Ratified February 27, 1951.

No person shall be elected to the office of the President more than twice, and no person who has held the office of President, or acted as President, for more than two years of a term to which some other person was elected President shall be elected to the office of the President more than once.

But this article shall not apply to any person holding the office of President when this article was proposed by the Congress, and shall not prevent any person who may be holding the office of President, or acting as President, during the term within which this article becomes operative from holding the office of President or acting as President during the remainder of such term.

This article shall be inoperative unless it shall have been ratified as an amendment to the Constitution by the legislatures of three-fourths of the several states within seven years from the date of its submission to the states by the Congress.

AMENDMENT XXIII

Passed by Congress June 16, 1960. Ratified March 29, 1961.

SECTION 1.   The District constituting the seat of Government of the United States shall appoint in such manner as the Congress may direct:

A number of electors of President and Vice President equal to the whole number of Senators and Representatives in Congress to which the District would be entitled if it were a State, but in no event more than the least populous state; they shall be in addition to those appointed by the states, but shall be considered, for the purpose of the election of President and Vice President, to be electors appointed by a state; and they shall meet in the District and perform such duties as provided by the twelfth article of amendment.

SECTION 2. The Congress shall have power to enforce this article by appropriate legislation.

Amendment XXIV

Passed by Congress August 27, 1962. Ratified January 23, 1964.

SECTION 1. The right of citizens of the United States to vote in any primary or other election for President or Vice President, for electors for President or Vice President, or for Senator or Representative in Congress, shall not be denied or abridged by the United States or any State by reason of failure to pay any poll tax or other tax.

SECTION 2. The Congress shall have the power to enforce this article by appropriate legislation.

Amendment XXV

Passed by Congress July 6, 1965. Ratified February 10, 1967.

SECTION 1. In case of the removal of the President from office or his death or resignation, the Vice President shall become President.

SECTION 2. Whenever there is a vacancy in the office of the

Vice President, the President shall nominate a Vice President who shall take the office upon confirmation by a majority vote of both houses of Congress.

SECTION 3. Whenever the President transmits to the President pro tempore of the Senate and the Speaker of the House of Representatives his written declaration that he is unable to discharge the powers and duties of his office, and until he transmits to them a written declaration to the contrary, such powers and duties shall be discharged by the Vice President as Acting President.

SECTION 4. Whenever the Vice President and a majority of either the principal officers of the executive departments, or of such other body as Congress may by law provide, transmit to the President pro tempore of the Senate and the Speaker of the House of Representatives their written declaration that the President is unable to discharge the powers and duties of his office, the Vice President shall immediately assume the powers and duties of the office of Acting President.

Thereafter, when the President transmits to the President pro tempore of the Senate and the Speaker of the House of Representatives his written declaration that no inability exists, he shall resume the powers and duties of his office unless the Vice President and a majority of either the principal officers of the executive department, or of such other body as Congress may by law provide, transmit within four days to the President pro tempore of the Senate and the Speaker of the House of Representatives their written declaration that the President is unable to discharge the powers and duties of his office. Thereupon Congress shall decide the issue, assembling within 48 hours for that purpose if not in session. If the Congress, within 21 days after receipt of the latter written declaration, or, if Congress is not in session, within 21 days after Congress is required to assemble, determines by two-thirds vote of both houses that the President is unable to discharge the powers and duties of his office, the Vice President shall continue to discharge the same as Acting President; otherwise, the President shall resume the powers and duties of his office.

Amendment XXVI

Passed by Congress March 23, 1971. Ratified June 30, 1971.

SECTION 1. The right of citizens of the United States, who are eighteen years of age or older, to vote shall not be denied or abridged by the United States or any state on account of age.

SECTION 2. The Congress shall have the power to enforce this article by appropriate legislation.

The Supreme Court and
the Constitution

★　　　★　　　★　　　★

Chief Justice Hughes once remarked that the Constitution means what the Supreme Court says it means, and Woodrow Wilson said that the Supreme Court resembles a constitutional convention in continuous session. As the court of last resort, the Supreme Court authoritatively interprets the Constitution. The buck stops here. Only the adoption of a constitutional amendment can override its decisions, and this has happened only four times in history: the Eleventh Amendment in 1798 reversed the 1793 decision in *Chisholm* v. *Georgia,* which permitted an individual to sue a state in federal court; the Fourteenth Amendment in 1868 reversed the 1857 decision in *Scott* v. *Sandford,* which held blacks not to be American citizens; the Sixteenth Amendment in 1913 reversed the 1895 decision in *Pollock* v. *Farmers' Loan and Trust Co.,* which prohibited a federal income tax; and the Twenty-sixth Amendment in 1971 reversed part of the 1970 decision in *Oregon* v. *Mitchell,* which denied Congress' power to enfranchise 18 to 20 year olds in state elections.

The Background of Judicial Review.　One searches the Constitution in vain for a statement granting the Supreme Court the power of judicial review. Article III does not list it among the subjects to which judicial power extends, while in Article VI, it is "the Judges in every State" whom the supremacy clause binds, with no mention of a federal court to review and make uniform the state courts' decisions. In the constitutional convention, the framers did debate the need for an authority with power to veto

67

legislative actions, but the proposal was voted down. How, then, was it possible for judicial review to become one of the most significant features of the American constitutional system?

An important influence was the Anglo-American legal system. The common law of England, which one commentator described as "the fruit of reason ripened by precedent," originated and developed in decisions of the courts, with the latest decision forming a precedent for the decision of similar cases that followed. The colonists brought the common law with them to America, where it became the everyday law for all the colonies. Another predisposing influence was the written charters and other documents that granted and limited the powers of colonial governments. The English Privy Council could disallow the acts of colonial legislatures and, through its judicial committee, it heard appeals from colonial courts. Theories of John Locke and Montesquieu on the desirability of limiting governmental powers, including those of the legislature, formed another important influence.

In Number 78 of *The Federalist* papers, Alexander Hamilton argued forcefully for judicial review, on the ground that the Constitution is superior to ordinary legislation and can be preserved only if the judiciary may void all legislative acts in conflict with its provisions. In 1798, Thomas Jefferson and James Madison advanced a different means of reviewing acts of Congress. Through the Kentucky and Virginia Resolutions, they called on the other states to declare the Alien and Sedition Acts unconstitutional. The Alien Act authorized the president to deport dangerous aliens; the Sedition Act made it a crime to bring the federal government into disrepute—its objective was to repress political opposition to the Federalist party. Although many states agreed that these laws did violate the Constitution, those north of Maryland also maintained that the federal courts, and not the states, are the proper organ to interpret the Constitution.

John Marshall. The establishment of judicial review was largely the work of John Marshall, who was appointed chief justice by President John Adams in 1801, just before Jefferson became president and his party took control of Congress. In *Marbury* v.

Madison (1803), Marshall wrote the opinion declaring unconstitutional a minor provision of the Judiciary Act of 1789 and thereby created a precedent for review of federal legislation. In *Fletcher* v. *Peck* (1810), the Court for the first time declared unconstitutional an act of a state legislature. In the large number of cases that followed, the Supreme Court sustained the exercise of federal power in some and invalidated state encroachments on the federal sphere in others. Among the most important were *M'Culloch* v. *Maryland* (1816), where Marshall exploited the language of the "necessary and proper" clause of Article I, section 8 to create the doctrine of implied federal powers, which substantially expanded the matters on which Congress might legislate; and *Gibbons* v. *Ogden* (1824), where Marshall defined the "commerce" that Congress could regulate extremely broadly. Both of these decisions are among the most important ever handed down.

Roger B. Taney.   The next chief justice, Roger B. Taney, who served from 1836 to 1864, had been President Andrew Jackson's attorney general and reflected Jacksonian attitudes toward states' rights and private property. During his tenure, the Court halted and in some respects reversed its stream of decisions strengthening and expanding federal authority. The Taney Court loosened the bonds of national supremacy, thereby permitting the states greater freedom of action. Neither the power given Congress to regulate commerce "among the several states" nor the clause prohibiting states from laws "impairing the Obligation of Contracts" precluded the states from regulating economic activities in a manner beneficial to their own residents. Taney's most famous—or infamous—decision, *Scott* v. *Sandford,* unsuccessfully attempted to settle the slavery controversy and, by declaring the Missouri Compromise unconstitutional, confirmed the precedent for judicial review that *Marbury* v. *Madison* had established.

The Post–Civil War Court.   During the Civil War, the Supreme Court lost prestige because military considerations tended to override judicial determinations of constitutional rights. During Reconstruction, the Court found itself in the middle of the constitutional struggle between the Radical Republicans, who controlled Congress, and President Andrew Johnson. The Court's size and jurisdiction were altered for partisan political purposes. As the war receded, the Court began to follow a laissez-faire course. Through the use of the due process clause in the Fourteenth Amendment, state efforts to regulate business and economic activities were declared unconstitutional. The Court, narrowly confining the scope of the interstate commerce clause, treated federal legislation similarly.

None of the chief justices possessed the leadership qualities that had made Marshall and Taney great. Some associate justices, however, were first-rate, including Samuel Miller, Stephen Field, and the first Justice Harlan, but they were a minority among others who had been attorneys for business interests. These, along with Justice Field, carried onto the Court their proclivities for laissez-faire economics. The demands of Greenbackers and Populists for political and social reforms affected the Court scarcely at all. Before the end of the nineteenth century, it had invalidated the federal income tax, defined the word "commerce" so as to prevent effective enforcement of the Sherman Antitrust Act, and washed its hands of racial matters. As far as a majority of the justices was concerned, the business of America was business and the purpose of the Court was to keep it that way.

The Early-Twentieth-Century Court.   The Court continued its pro-business stance into the twentieth century by formulating two constitutional doctrines that have since been overruled. Under "freedom of contract," the Court invalidated state and federal attempts to regulate wages and hours of work on the ground that they violated an individual's right to contract with his employer for the sale of his labor. Under "business affected with a public interest," it struck down legislation regulating businesses other than those that had traditionally been subject to public regulation, such as inns or public utilities. In its interpretations of constitutional commerce and taxing powers, the Court upheld laws benefiting business and agricultural interests, but was strangely unable to find a constitutional basis for outlawing child labor. (Compare *McCray* v. *United States* with *Bailey* v. *Drexel Furniture Co.*) Such able and forward-looking justices as Oliver Wendell Holmes and Louis Brandeis protested such interpretations and, by their dissenting opinions, prepared the way for new directions in constitutional law.

The New Deal. During the depression of the 1930s, President Franklin Roosevelt proposed and Congress enacted bold new legislation regulating many phases of American industry. It was inevitable that such legislation would come before the Supreme Court for review. The Court was then nearly equally divided in its disposition toward governmental regulation of the economy. Four justices—Willis Van Devanter, James McReynolds, George Sutherland, and Pierce Butler—staunchly supported laissez-faire economics. Three justices—Brandeis, Harlan Stone, and Benjamin Cardozo—believed that the Constitution should be interpreted in the light of existing economic conditions. Chief Justice Hughes usually sided with these three. Justice Owen Roberts initially sided with the four conservatives to make a majority that declared unconstitutional most of the early New Deal legislation.

After the Democratic landslide in the 1936 election, President Roosevelt proposed to increase the size of the Court by adding one new justice for each of the sitting justices who was over seventy years old, on the ground that the aged justices could not keep up with their work. The chief justice, however, presented convincing evidence that the Court's calendar was current. Notwithstanding presidential pressure, Congress refused to enact this "court-packing" plan, in large part because in the midst of the debate the Court began to uphold the more carefully considered and better drafted New Deal measures that Congress had passed to replace those the Court had previously voided.

Court packing thus became moot when, in the spring of 1937, Justice Roberts switched sides. By a margin of 5 to 4, the Court upheld several important New Deal statutes, among them the Social Security Act and legislation permitting labor to organize and bargain collectively. In the process, the meaning of interstate commerce was expanded to include all but purely local production and trade. Intrastate commerce and the Tenth Amendment lost nearly all significance in constitutional law. Although his court-packing plan failed, Roosevelt cemented the New Deal by filling seven vacancies on the high bench in the next four years, in addition to promoting Justice Stone to the chief justiceship.

The Warren Court.   The appointment of Earl Warren as chief justice in 1953 proved to be an event of special significance. Though he did not dominate the Court in the manner of Marshall, he exercised a steady and consistent influence. His most famous decision was *Brown* v. *Board of Education,* in which a unanimous Court declared compulsory racial segregation in public schools unconstitutional. During his sixteen-year tenure, the Court made the Bill of Rights more explicit than ever before. In numerous cases it expanded the meaning of freedom of speech and the press, required the states to observe nearly all the procedural guarantees in the Fourth through the Eighth Amendments, and restored population equality among the constituencies from which members of the House of Representatives and the two houses of the state legislatures are elected.

Commentators have termed the Warren Court "activist" because of its willingness to create new precedents to protect the rights of individuals. The "activist" label also fits the Marshall, Taney, post–Civil War, and other Courts equally well. They also created precedents to justify the policies they espoused. The fact that they did not particularly concern themselves with noneconomic civil rights and liberties does not make them less activist than their counterparts on the Warren Court. What the post–Civil War and the early-twentieth-century Courts did for business, the Warren Court did for individual freedom.

The Burger Court.   With the end of the Warren Court in 1969, membership changes caused the Court to turn in a conservative direction. The four justices nominated by President Nixon (Warren Burger, Harry Blackmun, Lewis Powell, and William Rehnquist) tended to vote together and to be joined by Byron White or Potter Stewart in numerous 5 to 4 decisions that differed from the positions of the Warren Court. With the retirement of William Douglas in 1975 and his replacement by John Stevens, the liberal majority of the 1960s was reduced to two: William Brennan and Thurgood Marshall. Opposite them sat the chief justice and Rehnquist. The other five justices occupied moderate to conservative positions.

On balance, the Burger Court drew the line between society as a whole and the rights of individuals a little more on the side of society. It opposed gender discrimination more than the Warren Court; a woman's right to an abortion and many rights afforded welfare recipients also resulted from decisions of the Burger Court. With regard to First Amendment freedoms, commercial advertising received constitutional protection, and parochial school efforts to gain governmental funding were defeated. Although the constitutionality of some forms of affirmative action was upheld, the Burger Court maintained the status quo generally on racial issues. Practical problems of law enforcement received substantial support, contrary to the behavior of the Warren Court majority.

The Rehnquist Court.   With the retirement of Chief Justice Burger at the end of the 1985–86 term, President Reagan nominated Justice Rehnquist, the Court's most conservative member, as Burger's replacement. To replace Rehnquist as associate justice the president selected Antonin Scalia, whom he had previously nominated to be a judge on the federal court of appeals for the District of Columbia. Inasmuch as Justice Scalia has a judicial track record similar to that of Burger, his appointment is not likely to alter the course of the Court's decisions. But other changes in the Court's personnel may affect the Court's policy orientation, depending on whether or not any new member(s) shares the attitudes and values of his predecessor.

How Cases Reach the Supreme Court.   Except for a handful of cases between states or between a state and the federal government (in which the Supreme Court functions as a trial court), the Court hears cases under its appellate jurisdiction: after they have been decided either by a lower federal court (usually a circuit court of appeals) or by the highest court in a state that has jurisdiction to try the particular case. The justices strictly limit access to the

Court, accepting for review no more than 1 to 2 percent of the cases losing litigants bring to their attention.

With a few relatively unimportant exceptions, the federal courts may decide only "federal questions"—those that pertain to the meaning of an act of Congress, a treaty of the United States, or a provision of the Constitution. Disputes about property, contracts, or personal injuries rarely have such a component. Hence, judicial resolution of these commonplace matters is the province of the state courts.

Most cases come to the Supreme Court on a writ of certiorari, which Congress authorized in 1925. A losing litigant may petition the Court for the writ and, if four justices approve, the Court will hear and decide the case. The usual grounds for granting the writ are the presence of a fundamental constitutional issue, an issue of general importance, an important private right, a federal statute not previously interpreted by the Court, or conflicting decisions by lower federal courts on a particular subject.

How the Court Operates.   The justices examine lower court records of the case, study the briefs of the attorneys who represent the litigants, and, if the petition to review the case is granted, hear oral argument. A majority vote determines the outcome of the case. If because of nonparticipation a tie vote results, the decision of the lower court stands. When he votes with the majority, the chief justice assigns the writing of the Court's opinion. Otherwise, the senior associate justice who voted with the majority makes the assignment. A justice who disagrees with the decision of the Court may write a dissenting opinion. If a justice agrees with the decision but not with the reasons given in the opinion of the Court, he may write an opinion concurring in the result. Such opinions, especially dissents, sometimes foreshadow changing interpretations of constitutional law.

Effect of Precedents.   Constitutional precedents set by the Supreme Court bind all lower courts, state and federal. The Supreme Court, interestingly enough, need not follow its own precedents, but it usually does so. Frequent overruling of precedents would make the law uncertain and the outcome of later cases unpredictable. On the other hand, slavish adherence to a specific line of precedent may retard adaptation of the law to changing circumstances and conditions. The Court has several options. It may follow precedent. It may distinguish the case before it from earlier cases and apply a different set of precedents to its resolution. It may specifically overrule the precedent. It may ignore the precedent, in effect overruling it *sub silentio*. It may label an issue a "political question" to be decided by Congress or the executive branch. Whatever it chooses to do, the Court's decision becomes the law of the land.

Selected Cases

★   ★   ★   ★

The following is a selection of major Supreme Court decisions. Without ignoring decisions of historical importance, we have given emphasis to cases of current significance. Under each topic the cases are arranged in chronological order so that the reader can follow the evolution of judicial policymaking and constitutional doctrine. A number of cases pertain to more than a single topic; in such instances, the case is cross-referenced to the heading under which it is summarized.

The topics themselves follow more or less the ordering of the major provisions in the Constitution. Beginning with judicial review, federal supremacy, and the separation of powers, we next consider the powers of the president, followed by those of Congress. Interspersed between them are implied powers and legislative apportionment and districting. The subject of Article III of the Constitution—the organization and jurisdiction of the federal judiciary—follows. An eclectic collection of topics pertaining to the states succeeds the four judicial subheads. Next comes the Bill of Rights and a myriad of topics focusing on the major guarantees contained therein. Three topics focus on the Thirteenth and Fourteenth Amendments, after which is a series of lengthy sections dealing with current issues pertaining to due process and equal protection. The topics conclude with the status and regulation of Indians and the matter of voting.

JUDICIAL REVIEW

***Marbury* v. *Madison* (1803).** The Court's first elaboration of the principle of judicial review. William Marbury applied directly to the Supreme Court, as provided by the Judiciary Act of 1789, for a writ of mandamus to compel Secretary of State James Madison to deliver to him his commission as justice of the peace in the District of Columbia, which had been signed and sealed—but not delivered—by the previous secretary of state, John Marshall. Two years later, Marshall, now chief justice, declared that Article III, section 2 of the Constitution allowed the Supreme Court to issue a writ of mandamus only under its appellate jurisdiction. Hence the provision of the Judiciary Act authorizing the writ of mandamus in an original proceeding, on which Marbury had relied, was invalid. The Constitution, said Marshall, is the fundamental law of the land; in cases of conflict between it and a statute, "an Act of the Legislature repugnant to the Constitution is void." Moreover, "it is emphatically the province and duty of the judicial department to say what the law is."

Judicial review is exercised not only by the Supreme Court but also by the lower federal courts and the state courts. Actions of the executive branches of government as well as those of Congress and the state legislatures are subject to judicial review.

***Martin* v. *Hunter's Lessee* (1816).** The Virginia Supreme Court alleged that the appellate jurisdiction of the United States Supreme Court did not extend to decisions of state courts and that a provision of the Judiciary Act of 1789 so extending it was unconstitutional. Virginia argued that like all the other states it was bound by the supremacy clause (Article VI, section 2) and, furthermore, that its judges were as competent as those sitting on the U.S. Supreme Court to determine whether a conflict existed between state and federal law. Marshall and his colleagues disagreed, holding that the Constitution "was ordained and established, not by the States in their sovereign capacities, but emphatically, as the preamble of the Constitution declares, by 'the people of the United States' "; that the Consitution "is crowded with provisions which restrain or annul the sovereignty of the States in some of the highest branches of their prerogatives" (see Article I, section 10); that exercise of federal judicial power over the judgments of state courts is not more dangerous than over state legislatures and executives; and that, in order to avoid differences among state courts in the interpretation of the Constitution and federal laws and treaties, it is necessary that there should be a reviewing authority to control and harmonize the "jarring and discordant judgments" that might be handed down by "judges of equal learning and integrity" in the different states.

This decision thus provides the basis for a uniform interpretation of federal law. Without it, the supreme court of each state would determine for itself the meaning of the Constitution, acts of Congress, and U.S. treaties. What constitutes due process of law, interstate commerce, the meaning of the First Amendment, and so on, would vary from state to state.

United States v. Nixon (1974). In a unanimous decision by the eight justices participating, the Court held that President Nixon must deliver to a U.S. district judge certain tapes of White House conversations subpoenaed for use in the criminal trials of former Nixon aides. Rejecting Nixon's contention, based on the doctrine of separation of powers, that he, as head of a coordinate branch of government, was not obliged to surrender the tapes, the Court reiterated the declaration in *Marbury* v. *Madison* that "it is emphatically the province and duty of the judicial department to say what the law is." The Court further stated that conversations between the president, his advisers, and others had no undifferentiated general immunity from judicial process; that the district judge, after listening to the tapes in private, could determine which portions, if any, contained sensitive military, diplomatic, or national security information, which need not be released. The importance of preserving confidentiality in White House conversations "must be balanced against the demonstrated need for evidence in a pending criminal trial."

FEDERAL SUPREMACY

United States v. *Peters* (1809).   A state legislature may not, by declaring that the decision of a lower federal court violated the Eleventh Amendment, impede the execution of the laws of the United States.

Ableman v. *Booth* (1859).   A Wisconsin court could not effect the release of a prisoner who was in the custody of a U.S. marshal for having violated federal law by helping a fugitive slave to escape. When a person is legally in federal custody for a federal offense and this fact has been communicated to state authorities, the state may not interfere.

Pennsylvania v. *Nelson* (1956).   Reversed a conviction under a state sedition law on the grounds that: (1) Congress, in passing the Smith Act and other internal security legislation, had evinced an intention to occupy the field of antisedition legislation to an extent that left no room for supplementary state legislation; (2) the federal interest in internal security is dominant and pervasive; and (3) a state program might conflict with federal objectives.

SEPARATION OF POWERS

Youngstown Sheet & Tube Co. v. *Sawyer* (1952).   The Court refused to uphold President Truman's seizure of steel mills in order to avert a strike that, he said, might hamper the Korean War effort by sharply reducing the supply of munitions. By a 6 to 3 vote and with seven separate opinions, the Court held that although Congress had considered granting the president power to seize strike-bound plants, it voted against doing so when it passed the Taft-Hartley Act. Nor could the Court find such authority in the clauses of Article II of the Constitution, which vest the president with executive power, make him commander in chief, and impose on him the duty to enforce federal law.

Train v. *New York City* (1975).   The president, as chief executive, has no power to countermand congressional authorization of funds for controlling and abating water pollution. Instead, the president must expend the full amounts authorized by Congress.

Nixon v. Administrator of General Services (1977). See under THE PRESIDENCY.

Immigration and Naturalization Service v. Chadha (1983). Legislation authorizing one house or committee of Congress to "veto" or annul action of the executive branch or an administrative agency, which action was authorized by duly enacted legislation, violates the procedures of Article I, section 7 of the Constitution. This article requires that *both* houses of Congress must pass a bill and present it to the president before it may take effect.

Bowsher v. Synar (1986). Held unconstitutional a key provision of the Gramm-Rudman deficit reduction act of 1985. The disallowed provision triggered automatic, across-the-board spending cuts designed to eliminate the federal budget deficit by 1991. By vesting the comptroller general with the executive power of estimating the size of the deficit and mandating annually the spending reductions necessary to meet the deficit reduction target, Congress violated the doctrine of separation of powers. The reason: The comptroller general is an agent of Congress whom it may remove from office. As such, he may not exercise executive power. Justice White, in dissent, criticized the majority's decision, observing that the comptroller is "one of the most independent officers in the entire federal establishment."

THE PRESIDENCY

Kendall v. United States (1838). An officer, in this case the postmaster general, may not refuse to perform a duty imposed on him by an act of Congress, even though the president has ordered him not to perform it. Congress may assign to any executive officer any duty it may think proper that is not repugnant to rights protected by the Constitution. The majority opinion stated: "To contend that the obligation imposed on the President to see the laws faithfully executed implies a power to forbid their execution is a novel construction of the Constitution and is entirely inadmissible."

***Mississippi* v. *Johnson* (1867).** A decision arising from the attempt of Mississippi to obtain an injunction to prevent the president from enforcing one of the reconstruction acts on the ground that the law was unconstitutional. The Court held that the president's responsibility to enforce the laws is not a mere ministerial duty, in which nothing is left to his discretion, but is rather an executive and political duty. Therefore, an injunction may not be issued against the president to restrain him from enforcing a law.

***In re Neagle* (1890).** The attorney general assigned a U.S. deputy marshal (Neagle) as a bodyguard for Justice Field, whose life had been threatened. While Field was on circuit duty in California, the marshal killed an assailant who was threatening the justice. A California court indicted Neagle for murder. Under federal law he could be released by writ of habeas corpus from state authority only if he had been acting under a law of the United States. No act of Congress authorized the attorney general to assign a bodyguard to a justice. However, the Court held that the writ could issue on the basis of an executive order, because the president's duty to execute the law includes the implied power to protect government officials while on duty.

***In re Debs* (1895).** Upheld a federal injunction against striking Pullman Company employees who had halted rail transportation in the Chicago area and sustained President Cleveland in sending in troops when the injunction was disobeyed, though the Illinois governor protested the president's action. The Court asserted that "the strong arm of the national Government may be put forth to brush away all obstructions to the freedom of interstate commerce or the transportation of the mails."

***Nixon* v. *Administrator of General Services* (1977).** Rejected former President Nixon's claim to his presidential papers after Congress had provided that the General Services Administration should determine which papers were public and which should be returned to him as private. Nixon based his claim on separation of powers (*q.v.*), presidential privilege, and his right to privacy. By a 7 to 2 vote, the Court held that the test for violation of separation of powers is whether one branch unduly disrupts another. It held that nothing contained in the act of Congress was unduly disruptive; that the act's screening process was "a very limited intrusion" for which adequate justification had been shown; and that Nixon's privacy was only slightly infringed, whereas the justification for the screening process was substantial.

Butz v. Economou (1978). Although federal officials may not be sued for mistakes of judgment, they are personally liable for acting in a way that they know, or should know, violates a person's constitutional rights. The Court majority, however, excepted from this qualified immunity govermental attorneys, judges, and other officials whose duties involve adjudication. These persons are absolutely immune from suit for injuries resulting from their official actions.

Nixon v. Fitzgerald (1982). No president may be sued for damages for any official action he takes while in office.

THE REMOVAL POWER

Myers v. United States (1926). Declared unconstitutional the Tenure of Office Act of 1876, which required the consent of the Senate for the removal of certain classes of postmasters. The Court held that the president may remove at pleasure any officer appointed by himself and the Senate under the executive powers vested in him by Article II. He is responsible for the execution of the laws, and he can execute the laws only through subordinates. He must have the power, therefore, to remove subordinates in whom he lacks confidence. Limited by *Humphrey's Executor* v. *United States.*

Humphrey's Executor (Rathbun) v. United States (1935). The Court limited the scope of *Myers* v. *United States* by denying the president power to remove quasi-legislative and quasi-judicial officers when Congress made other provisions for their removal. As a result, Congress acted constitutionally when, in creating the Federal Trade Commission, it specified that the president could remove a commissioner only for inefficiency, neglect of duty, or malfeasance in office. The duties of such officers are not purely executive and, consequently, they are not exclusively subject to presidential control. The majority opinion stated: "It is quite evident that one who holds his office only during the pleasure of another cannot be depended upon to maintain an attitude of independence against the latter's will."

Wiener v. *United States* **(1958).**   Even though Congress had not limited the president's power to remove members of the War Claims Commission, their functions are intrinsically judicial; hence the president may not remove them at will, but only for cause.

FOREIGN AFFAIRS

Foster v. *Neilson* **(1829).**   The Court refused to review the merits of a dispute over land grants in territory east of the Mississippi River claimed by both Spain and the United States. The Spanish grant had been made in 1804. The United States later claimed the territory as part of the Louisiana Purchase and occupied it by force. The Court said that decisions of the president and Congress bind the judiciary in all matters affecting the rights of the United States in foreign affairs.

United States v. *Curtiss-Wright Corp.* **(1936).**   Upheld an arms embargo imposed by the president under authority given to him by joint resolution of Congress. According to the Court, "The president is the sole organ of the Federal government in the field of international relations—a power which does not require as a basis for its exercise an act of Congress, but which . . . , like every other governmental power, must be exercised in subordination to the applicable provisions of the Constitution."

TREATIES AND EXECUTIVE AGREEMENTS

Head Money Cases (1884).   Sustained an act of Congress that levied a tax on steamship companies amounting to a small sum per capita on every immigrant brought to the United States, even though some of these immigrants came from countries with which the United States had treaties guaranteeing their free admission.

The Court held treaties and statutes to be of equal weight. Hence if a self-executory treaty (one that requires no statute for its enforcement) and an act of Congress conflict, the one more recently enacted prevails.

Missouri v. Holland (1920). Sustained a federal statute to enforce a treaty with Great Britain for the mutual protection of migratory birds flying between the United States and British possessions in North America. Migratory birds involve a "a national interest of very nearly the first magnitude," the Court said, which only "national action in concert with that of another power" can protect. The birds are "only transitorily within the State" and have "no permanent habitat therein." Lower federal courts had invalidated a federal statute for the protection of migratory birds, which antedated the treaty, as a usurpation of the reserved powers of the states and an encroachment on their property rights.

United States v. Belmont (1937). Sustained an executive agreement that President Franklin Roosevelt, without consulting the Senate, entered into when he established diplomatic relations with the Soviet Union in 1933. The Court ruled that recognition, the establishment of diplomatic relations, and the agreement assigning American assets of a former Russian corporation to the U.S.S.R. were all part of a single transaction, within the power of the president to make, and that he spoke as the "sole organ" of the government in the transaction. To the objection that the Soviet Union had acquired the assets by confiscation, in violation of New York law, the Court replied that by recognizing the Soviet Union the United States accepted all actions of the U.S.S.R. pertaining to its own citizens, and that the executive agreement overrode conflicting state laws.

Reid v. Covert (1957). An international agreement whereby American servicemen and their dependents who committed crimes on British soil were to be tried by American courts did not authorize the United States to use a military tribunal to try the wife of a soldier. She was not a member of "the land and naval forces," for whose regulation Congress may provide in Article I, section 8; rather, she was a civilian, under the Fifth and Sixth Amendments, answerable to indictment only by a grand jury and entitled to trial by jury. The Court ruled that "no agreement with a foreign nation can confer power on the Congress, or on any other branch of Government, which is free from the restraints of the Constitution."

THE PRESIDENT AS COMMANDER IN CHIEF

The Prize Cases (1863). Four cases concerning vessels captured while running a naval blockade that President Lincoln had imposed by proclamation on Southern ports shortly after the Civil War began. The Court sustained the president's action, saying: "If a war be made by invasion of a foreign nation, the President is not only authorized but bound to resist force, by force. He . . . is bound to accept the challenge without waiting for any special legislative authority. And whether the hostile party be a foreign invader, or States organized in rebellion, it is none the less a war." Congress later enacted legislation ratifying the president's proclamation.

***Ex parte Milligan* (1866).** A civilian was convicted of fomenting insurrection and other treasonable activities by a military commission sitting at Indianapolis in 1864. He applied to a U.S. circuit court for a writ of habeas corpus. On appeal, Milligan was held to have been unlawfully convicted because President Lincoln had acted unconstitutionally in establishing military commissions in places where the civil courts were open and their processes unobstructed. Such action was permissible only in an actual theater of war where civil courts were not functioning.

***Ex parte Quirin* (1942).** Seven Germans who landed secretly on American shores during World War II for the purpose of committing sabotage were tried and sentenced by a military commission after their capture. The Court determined that the military commission had been properly constituted; that though the saboteurs were captured and tried in a district where courts were open (see *ex parte Milligan*, above), they were nonetheless subject to military jurisdiction as "unlawful belligerents" under the laws of war. A Sixth Amendment right to jury trial does not apply since that guarantee pertains to civil and not to military courts.

***Korematsu* v. *United States* (1944).**   Korematsu, a native-born citizen of Japanese ancestry, was one of 112,000 Japanese-Americans, 70,000 of whom were U.S. citizens, who were summarily removed from their homes in designated West Coast areas and shipped to inland "relocation centers" in accordance with a 1942 executive order. The Court sustained Korematsu's removal because "the properly constituted military authorities" feared an invasion of the West Coast and decided that military necessity required the removal of all persons of Japanese origin from the area. The decision—still valid law—seemed to constitutionalize guilt by association. Justice Jackson pointed out in dissent: Korematsu "has been convicted . . . of being present in the state whereof he is a citizen, near the place where he was born, and where all his life he has lived . . . merely because [he] is the son of parents as to whom he had no choice, and belongs to a race from which there is no way to resign."

Forty years later, a federal district court vacated Korematsu's conviction because government attorneys had failed to reveal to the Supreme Court key evidence that contradicted the military's claim that the Japanese-Americans posed a threat to national security.

***Toth* v. *Quarles* (1955).**   The Court held unconstitutional an act of Congress requiring discharged servicemen to be tried by courts martial for crimes allegedly committed during active duty. The Court said that such a requirement would deprive veterans of the safeguards enjoyed by other civilians under Article III of the Constitution and would encroach on the jurisdiction of the regular courts.

WAR POWERS*

Selective Draft Law Cases (1918).   The Court supported the compulsory features of the Selective Service Act of 1917, which

*See also THE PRESIDENT AS COMMANDER IN CHIEF.

required young men to register for military service. The power of Congress to raise and support armies is separate and distinct from its power to call the states' militia into federal service. The constitutional power to raise armies includes the power to compel military service. Such service is a citizen's obligation to his government and is sanctioned by numerous precedents. Subsequent cases emphasized and extended this decision.

***Block* v. *Hirsh* (1921).**   Sustained state and federal emergency rent laws enacted at the close of World War I. The legislation, which fixed rents and temporarily extended leases, was held to be consistent with due process on the theory that the wartime emergency had clothed the relationship between landlord and tenant with a preponderant public interest and had made that relationship temporarily subject to the same sort of regulatory power that government may exert over the rates and services of public utilities.

***Ashwander* v. *Tennessee Valley Authority* (1936).**   The case concerned a contract for the sale to a private company of surplus electric power generated at a government dam. The Court upheld the peacetime maintenance of the dam and the hydroelectric installations constructed in World War I, under both the power to improve navigation and the power to provide for the future supply of munitions. It upheld the acquisition by the Tennessee Valley Authority of transmission lines for the distribution and sale of its electric power on the principle that, if the government owns property, Congress, acting in the public interest, may determine the manner and conditions of its disposition.

***Woods* v. *Miller* (1948).**   Sustained the Housing and Rent Control Act of 1947. Congress, even after the cessation of hostilities, may remedy conditions resulting from wartime mobilization of men and materiel, under its war powers and the necessary and proper clause of Article I, section 8.

THE POWER TO PARDON

***Ex parte Garland* (1867).**   The Court declared unconstitutional, as a bill of attainder, an act of Congress that required lawyers practicing in federal courts to take an oath that they had never voluntarily borne arms against the United States or given aid to its enemies. Garland, though pardoned by President Johnson for serving in both houses of the Confederate Congress, could not take the oath. The Court held that under Article II, section 2 a full pardon "releases the punishment and blots out of existence the guilt so that in the eye of the law the offender is as innocent as if he had never committed the offense." The pardoning power extends to every offense against the law and may be exercised before legal proceedings commence, while they are pending, or after conviction and judgment.

Ex parte Grossman (1925).   Ruled that the president may pardon and remit a sentence imposed by a federal court for criminal contempt on the ground that numerous precendents for such pardons exist in England and the United States. They are especially useful, the Court stated, when sentences are imposed "without the restraining influence of a jury and without many of the guarantees which the Bill of Rights offers to protect the individual against unjust conviction." But a pardon "can only be granted for a contempt fully completed." It cannot stop "coercive measures" to enforce rights of a complainant.

Schick v. Reed (1974).   The president may commute a death sentence to life imprisonment and constitutionally attach thereto a condition of no parole.

IMPLIED POWERS

M'Culloch v. Maryland (1819).   The classic exposition of the doctrine of implied powers, which allows for a loose, or broad, construction of the powers delegated to the federal government. The case arose from the refusal of the cashier of the Baltimore branch of the Bank of the United States to pay a tax levied by Maryland on notes issued by the bank. Chief Justice Marshall declared for the Court that the last clause of Article I, section 8 gives Congress the means to carry out its expressly granted powers, and that the Bank was "necessary and proper" to taxing, borrowing, and conveying funds for the support of armies. "Let the end be legitimate, let it be within the scope of the Constitution, and all means which are appropriate, which are plainly adapted to that end, which are not prohibited, but consist with the letter and spirit of the Constitution, are constitutional."

Moreover, Maryland could not tax the Bank because such a use of the state's taxing power threatens the supremacy of the federal government in matters committed to its jurisdiction. "The States have no power, by taxation or otherwise, to retard, impede, burden, or in any manner control, the operation of the constitutional laws enacted by Congress to carry into execution the powers vested in the general government."

LEGISLATIVE APPORTIONMENT AND DISTRICTING

Colegrove v. *Green* (1946). A suit to compel reapportionment of congressional districts presents a nonjusticiable political question. Though the rural-dominated Illinois legislature had not changed the boundaries of the state's congressional districts since 1901, and though great population discrepancies existed, the Court declined to intervene because the justices deemed the Court ought not to become involved in partisan political disputes; it could not itself redistrict the state, and the Constitution in Article I, section 4 vests authority for dealing with such problems in Congress itself. Overruled by *Wesberry* v. *Sanders* (see below).

Baker v. *Carr* (1962). Invalidated a Tennessee legislative apportionment that had remained unaltered for over sixty years despite losses of population in many counties and large increases in others. Rejecting the rule of *Colegrove* v. *Green* (see above), the Court held that the equitable apportionment of voters among legislative districts is a justiciable, rather than a political, question, and that when the apportionment is inequitable, courts may provide relief.

Wesberry v. *Sanders* (1964). Overruled *Colegrove* v. *Green* (see above). Invalidated the unequal apportionment of Georgia's congressional districts on the ground that since every voter is equal to every other voter, the districts from which members of Congress are chosen must be as nearly equal in population as practicable.

Reynolds v. *Sims* (1964). Extended the principle of "one person, one vote" to apply to the apportionment of seats in both houses of a state's legislature.

Kirkpatrick v. *Preisler* (1969). In dividing a state into congressional districts, the state legislature must make all districts equal in population or justify the variance.

Hadley v. *Junior College District* (1970). Each district from which government officials are chosen must contain a population as nearly equal as practicable to every other district. This one-person, one-vote principle applies to all elected officials—local as well as state—who perform "public functions" and not only to those holding legislative office.

Mahan v. *Howell* (1973). Greater variation in population (in this case, 16.4 percent) between the largest and smallest state legislative districts is more permissible than variation in congressional districts.

Salyer Land Co. v. *Tulare Water District* (1973). Upheld weighted voting of elected officials in special-purpose governmental bodies that "disproportionately affect" a subset of the total population. Here a local water storage district chose its directors on the basis of one vote for every $100 worth of real estate an individual owned.

LEGISLATIVE MEMBERSHIP AND PREROGATIVES

Bond v. *Floyd* (1966). The lower house of the Georgia legislature violated Julian Bond's First Amendment right to freedom of speech when it refused to accept him as a member because of his utterances in opposition to the Vietnam War.

Powell v. *McCormack* (1969). The House of Representatives may not add to the constitutional qualifications of age, residence, and citizenship or exclude by a majority vote a duly elected member who possesses them. Adam Clayton Powell had been denied his seat because of charges that in previous sessions of Congress he had submitted false expense accounts and had misused committee funds. The residents of a congressional district are entitled to representation, the Court ruled, and this right can constitutionally be overridden only by a two-thirds vote of the House to expel.

Gravel v. United States (1972). The "speech or debate" clause of Article I, section 6 allows the legislative aide of a member of Congress to share the member's immunity from being "questioned in any other place" than in the legislative chamber or committee. But when arrangements are made for private publication of government documents (here, the "Pentagon Papers"), the aide must tell a grand jury what he knows about how allegedly stolen documents came into the possession of a member of Congress.

Doe v. McMillan (1973). The speech or debate clause absolutely immunizes the members and staff of a congressional committee who prepare and disseminate a derogatory report. However, a member of Congress may not with impunity repeat libelous statements from a report in circumstances that are "not an essential part of the legislative process."

Hutchinson v. Proxmire (1979). The speech, or debate, clause does not apply to congressional newsletters or press releases. The "informing function" that the clause protects concerns the means that representatives and senators use to inform one another, not to communications to a member's constituents.

LEGISLATIVE INVESTIGATIONS

Kilbourn v. Thompson (1881). Congress has no authority to inquire into matters about which it has no power to legislate.

Watkins v. United States (1957). Reversed the conviction of a labor leader who, when called before the House Committee on Un-American Activities, freely answered questions concerning his own involvement with the Communist party but refused to name other persons who long ago had severed their party connections. When Congress creates a committee it must spell out the committee's jurisdiction so that witnesses and reviewing authorities can determine whether questions asked are pertinent. "Investigations conducted solely for the personal aggrandizement of the investigators, or to 'punish' those investigated are indefensible," the Court stated. "The Bill of Rights is applicable to all investigations."

Barenblatt v. *United States* **(1959).**   By a 5 to 4 vote, the Court held that a college teacher's academic freedom under the First Amendment properly pertained to the classroom but did not protect him from the consequences of refusing to answer pertinent questions about his knowledge of Communist influence and his association with Communists on American college campuses when such questions were asked under the undoubted power of Congress to inquire into alleged Communist infiltration into the field of education.

THE POWER TO TAX AND SPEND

Pollock v. *Farmers' Loan and Trust Co.* **(1894, 1895).**   Declared unconstitutional an act of Congress imposing an income tax without apportionment among the states (see Article I, section 9) on the ground that a tax on land is a direct tax and a tax on the income derived from land is indistinguishable from a tax on the land itself. In 1895, the Court applied the same principle to the income from stocks and bonds. Ratification of the Sixteenth Amendment canceled both decisions.

McCray v. *United States* **(1904).**   The Court refused to inquire into the motives of Congress when it imposed a tax of ten cents per pound on oleomargarine artificially colored to imitate butter and only one-fourth cent per pound on uncolored margarine. Opponents claimed that the tax was meant to achieve regulatory and not fiscal ends, and that it destroyed property rights without due process. The majority, however, said that the act "on its face" is a revenue measure.

Bailey v. *Drexel Furniture Co.* **(1922).**   Declared unconstitutional an act of Congress imposing a 10 percent tax on the net profits of any business that knowingly employed children under certain specified ages. The Court ruled that the word "knowingly" applied to criminal law, not to taxation, and that the tax was not a bona fide revenue measure but rather a police regulation. As such, it ran afoul of the Tenth Amendment by invading matters reserved to the states. Effectively overruled by *Mulford* v. *Smith* (see below).

United States v. Butler (1936).   Invalidated the first Agricultural Adjustment Act because coercive federal regulation of farm production and prices infringes on powers reserved to the states. The court ruled that processing taxes are an integral part of an unconstitutional scheme of regulation and furthermore that the revenue derived from the taxes, which was used to subsidize farmers, could not be sustained under the general welfare provision of the first clause of Article I, section 8.

Social Security Cases. [*Helvering* v. *Davis* (1937) and *Steward Machine Co.* v. *Davis* (1937)].   The Court upheld the constitutionality of federal taxes on employers and employees in certain businesses to finance the joint federal-state system of unemployment compensation, special assistance to wage earners and others, and the federal old-age insurance program of the Social Security Act of 1935. The five-member majority decreed that Congress had properly regarded social insecurity as a national problem that could be attacked nationally; that the cooperative federal-state features of the social security system do not violate the Tenth Amendment or coerce the states into abandoning their governmental responsibilities. The proceeds from the taxes were to be spent to promote the general welfare.

Mulford v. Smith (1939).   The Court effectively overruled *United States* v. *Butler* (see above) and sustained the second Agricultural Adjustment Act. Congress might constitutionally regulate the flow of an agricultural commodity to the interstate market in order to foster, protect, and conserve commerce or "to prevent the flow of commerce from working harm to the people of the nation."

THE SCOPE OF THE COMMERCE POWER

Gibbons v. Ogden (1824).   In a classic opinion, Chief Justice Marshall defined Congress' power to regulate foreign and interstate commerce to embrace every species of commercial inter-course, including navigation between the United States and foreign nations as well as every commercial transaction that does not wholly occur within the boundaries of a single state. The power does not stop at a state's boundary but extends to activity within a state that affects other states.

After the Civil War until the mid-1930s, the Court tended to adhere to definitions of interstate commerce markedly more restrictive than Marshall's. Not until the eve of World War II did the Court allow Congress to use the commerce power as a regulatory tool, as the decisions summarized under FEDERAL REGULATION OF BUSINESS and FEDERAL REGULATION OF LABOR illustrate.

Wickard v. *Filburn* (1942). An Ohio farmer who planted twenty-three acres of wheat for his own consumption, exceeding the quota set by the secretary of agriculture, exerted "a substantial economic effect on interstate commerce." He thereby made himself liable for penalties imposed by the Agricultural Adjustment Act of 1938. This decision well illustrates the economic reach of the constitutional commerce power.

Katzenbach v. *McClung* (1964). The 1964 Civil Rights Act outlaws race discrimination in places of public accommodation that affect interstate commerce. Without dissent, the justices agreed that the statute applied to a family-owned restaurant, not patronized by interstate travelers, merely because $70,000 worth of food consumed on the premises had previously moved in interstate commerce.

FEDERAL REGULATION OF BUSINESS

United States v. *E. C. Knight Co.* (1895). The Sherman Antitrust Act did not apply to a combination of four Pennsylvania companies that had a virtual monopoly of sugar refining because (1) manufacture precedes commerce and is not a part of it, (2) interstate commerce does not commence until goods begin their final movement from one state to another, and (3) the manufacturing monopoly in this case had no "direct" effect on interstate commerce. Effectively overruled by *National Labor Relations Board* v. *Jones and Laughlin Steel Corp* (see below).

Northern Securities Co. v. United States (1904). The first successful prosecution under the Sherman Act. The Court ordered the dissolution of a holding company that controlled the Great Northern and the Northern Pacific Railroads on the grounds that it lessened competition and restrained interstate commerce.

Swift & Co. v. United States (1905). Affirmed the power of Congress to punish conspiracies in restraint of trade among buyers and sellers in the Chicago stockyards. The Court stated that in the habitual course of commerce, livestock originating in one state paused at the Chicago stockyards only long enough to find a buyer before being shipped to another state. Therefore, they had remained within the "current," or stream, of commerce.

Standard Oil Co. v. United States (1911). The Court ordered the dissolution of the Standard Oil Company of New Jersey, not because of its huge size but because it had used its economic power through pricing and other manipulative policies to restrain trade unreasonably.

Schechter Poultry Co. v. United States (1935). A unanimous Court declared the National Industrial Recovery Act unconstitutional because it delegated legislative powers to the president and attempted, under the guise of the commerce power in Article I, section 8, to regulate aspects of a business—the slaughtering and sale of locally grown poultry—that falls within the jurisdiction of the states.

National Labor Relations Board v. Jones and Laughlin Steel Corp. (1937). The Court abandoned the doctrine of *United States* v. *E. C. Knight Co.* (see above) that manufacturing is not commerce. It upheld provisions of the Wagner Act forbidding unfair labor practices that affect interstate commerce. (The case concerned clerical employees who had been dismissed for union-organizing activities.) Although the defendant steel company was not directly engaged in transportation, the successful conduct of its far-flung business depended on the free flow of interstate commerce to furnish it with raw materials and to market its products in other states and in foreign countries; hence the prohibition of unfair labor practices properly protects and promotes interstate commerce.

FEDERAL REGULATION OF LABOR

***Adair* v. *United States* (1905).**   Invalidated a federal statute outlawing in interstate commerce employment those contracts under which a worker agreed not to join a union (yellow-dog contract). The Court declared the law a violation of the due process clause of the Fifth Amendment because it abridged freedom of contract. Employer and employee "have equality of right, and any legislation that disturbs that equality is an arbitrary interference with the liberty of contract." Subsequently overruled.

***Loewe* v. *Lawlor* (1908).**   The famous Danbury Hatters' case. A nationwide boycott by a labor union of hats manufactured by non-union shops was ruled to restrain trade under the Sherman Antitrust Act. The Clayton Act of 1914 nullified this decision by exempting labor unions from the operation of the Sherman Act.

***Wilson* v. *New* (1917).**   Upheld the constitutionality of the Adamson Act, which provided for an eight-hour day and appropriate wage standards for interstate railroad workers.

***Hammer* v. *Dagenhart* (1918).**   By a 5 to 4 vote declared unconstitutional a federal law prohibiting the interstate shipment of goods made in factories employing children. The law, said the majority, is not a bona fide regulation of commerce but an effort to control the conditions of employment and manufacture within the states. Goods produced by child labor are not deleterious in themselves and are indistinguishable from those made by adults. Overruled by *United States* v. *Darby* (see below).

***Adkins* v. *Children's Hospital* (1923).**   Declared the minimum wage law of the District of Columbia unconstitutional. The law violates the rights of the parties freely to contract with one another. It establishes standards of enforcement that are "too vague and fatally uncertain," requires employers to pay a minimum wage whether or not the employee was worth that much, and is "so clearly the product of a naked, arbitrary exercise of power that it cannot be allowed to stand under the Constitution," the Court stated. Overruled fourteen years later by *West Coast Hotel Co.* v. *Parrish*. See under STATE LABOR REGULATION.

United States v. Darby (1941). Sustained provisions of the Fair Labor Standards Act of 1938 that fixed maximum hours and minimum wages for most employees and barred from interstate commerce the shipment of goods manufactured in violation of its provisions. According to the Court: ". . . while manufacturing is not of itself interstate commerce, the shipment of manufactured goods interstate is such commerce." Overruled and repudiated the reasoning of *Hammer* v. *Dagenhart* (see above).

STATE LABOR REGULATION

Holden v. Hardy (1898). Upheld a Utah law limiting underground miners to an eight-hour day. The majority saw no reason to doubt the legislature's judgment that working long hours at such an occupation is detrimental to health. In response to the argument that the law violates a worker's right to contract his labor, the Court replied that "the state still retains an interest in his welfare, however reckless he may be."

Lochner v. New York (1905). By a 5 to 4 vote, invalidated a state law limiting bakers to a ten-hour day, sixty-hour week. Baking is not an unhealthy occupation; therefore the state may not regulate it. The statute unreasonably interfered with freedom of contract, which the due process clause of the Fourteenth Amendment protects. Modified by *Muller* v. *Oregon* (see below) and subsequently overruled.

Muller v. Oregon (1908). Modified *Lochner* v. *New York* (see above) by upholding an Oregon statute forbidding the employment of women in certain industries for more than ten hours per day, apparently on the ground that women require legislative protection because they are less able than men to endure sustained labor.

West Coast Hotel Co. v. Parrish (1937). The Court reversed earlier decisions, such as *Adkins* v. *Children's Hospital* (see under

FEDERAL REGULATION OF LABOR), by upholding, 5 to 4, minimum wage legislation for women. The majority rejected arguments that such legislation violates the due process clause of the Fourteenth Amendment, stating that "the liberty safeguarded is liberty in a social organization which requires the protection of law against the evils which menace the health, safety, morals and welfare of the people."

This decision signaled the end of the Court's use of the due process clause as a means of preventing the state legislatures from passing regulations incompatible with the principles of laissez-faire economics. Hereafter, states were free to regulate prices and working conditions, establish minimum wages and maximum hours of work, and ban child labor without fear that they would run afoul of federal judges. This decision thus did for state economic regulation what *National Labor Relations Board* v. *Jones and Laughlin Steel Corp.,* decided two weeks later, did for federal economic regulation. See under FEDERAL REGULATION OF BUSINESS.

STATE REGULATION OF INTERSTATE COMMERCE

Cooley v. Board of Wardens (1851). The Court formulated the doctrine that Congress' commerce power is not exclusive, and that where a uniform national rule is not required, the states may apply their own regulations to foreign and interstate commerce. (Here the issue concerned the piloting of ships in the port of Philadelphia.) Such regulations remain valid until such time as Congress supersedes them.

Shreveport Rate Case (*Houston E. & W. Texas R. Co.* v. *United States,* 1914). The Texas Railway Commission fixed unreasonably low rates between distributing centers in Texas and points near the state's borders, thereby putting at a disadvantage shippers in other states whose rates were fixed by the Interstate Commerce Commission. The Court ordered the Texas commission to end the discrimination.

South Carolina Highway Dept. v. Barnwell Bros (1938). In the absence of congressional regulation, a state may impose limits on the weight and width of motor vehicles traveling interstate over its highways. The states and their local subdivisions have built the highways and are responsible for their safe use, and the regulation in question does not discriminate against interstate commerce.

Southern Pacific Co. v. Arizona (1945). Invalidated a law that prohibited railroad train lengths of more than fourteen passenger cars or seventy freight cars. The burden on interstate commerce outweighed the law's problematical advantages as a safety measure inasmuch as longer trains operate safely in states other than Arizona.

Huron Portland Cement Co. v. Detroit (1960). A municipality may apply its smoke abatement ordinance to ships operating in interstate commerce, though the ships' boilers and equipment have been federally inspected and licensed. The regulation is valid because it looks to the health of the local community and imposes no discriminatory burden on interstate commerce. Federal legislation, by contrast, concerns maritime safety and does not preempt the field to the exclusion of local police regulations.

Kassel v. Consolidated Freightways (1981). Although reluctant to invalidate state regulations concerning highway safety, the Court ruled that Iowa unconstitutionally burdened interstate commerce by banning double tractor-trailer trucks from its roads. The six justices in the majority could not agree on an opinion, but four of them did observe that Iowa's "real concern was not safety but an effort to limit the use of its highways by deflecting some through traffic" to neighboring states.

THE TENTH AMENDMENT AS A LIMITATION ON FEDERAL REGULATION

Maryland v. Wirtz (1968). Federal wage and hour legislation applies to public school and hospital employees. In exercising its powers, stated the Court, the federal government "may override countervailing state interests," regardless of whether they are " 'governmental' or 'proprietary' in character."

National League of Cities v. Usery (1976). Declared unconstitutional congressional extension of minimum wage laws to the employees of states and their subdivisions. The Tenth Amendment prevents Congress from using the commerce power to interfere with any state activity the performance of which may be characterized as an "attribute of sovereignty," according to the majority opinion. Besides increased cost, such laws burden the states and interfere with their right to manage their own affairs. Overruled by *Garcia* v. *San Antonio Metropolitan Transit Authority* (see below).

United Transportation Union v. Long Island Rail Road Co. (1982). The Tenth Amendment does not prohibit application of the Railway Labor Act to a state-owned railroad engaged in interstate commerce. The operation of a railroad is not an activity in which states typically engage. Hence, the Court ruled, the federal law does not regulate the "states as states"; neither does it address a matter that is indisputably an attribute of state sovereignty.

Garcia v. San Antonio Metropolitan Transit Authority (1985). Justice Blackmun, who provided the key vote in *National League of Cities* v. *Usery* (see above), switched to the other side and wrote the Court's opinion overruling *Usery*. Application of federal wage and hour provisions to employees of a city-owned transportation system "contravened no affirmative limit on Congress' power under the commerce clause," stated the majority opinion. One may assume that the Court has come full circle and now reoccupies the position it took in *Maryland* v. *Wirtz* (see above).

JUDICIAL ORGANIZATION

Ex parte Bakelite Corporation (1929). Differentiated the constitutional courts created under Article III from the so-called legislative courts that have specialized jurisdictions to adjudicate claims, settle disputes over customs duties and patents, and administer justice in U.S. territories created by Congress under Articles I and IV of the Constitution. In creating legislative courts,

Congress is not bound by the limitations of Article III concerning jurisdiction or the tenure and compensation of federal judges.

Glidden Co. v. Zdanok (1962).   After an act of Congress had provided that the Court of Claims and the Court of Customs and Patent Appeals should become constitutional courts under Article III, the Supreme Court ruled that judges of these specialized courts may not be assigned to sit on district or circuit courts, the regular constitutional courts, because they lack life tenure.

Northern Pipeline Construction Co. v. Marathon Pipe Line Co. (1982).   The federal bankruptcy courts, established in 1978, may not constitutionally exercise all the power Congress provided them. Judges who exercise Article III jurisdiction, as bankruptcy judges did under the act of Congress, must also be provided the salary and tenure protections of Article III, which bankruptcy judges do not have.

JURISDICTION OF THE FEDERAL COURTS

Chisholm v. Georgia (1793).   Supreme Court jurisdiction over controversies "between a State and citizens of another State" included the power to hear and decide a case brought by Chisholm, a citizen of South Carolina, against the state of Georgia to obtain compensation for property taken during the Revolutionary War. This decision alarmed the states that had outstanding debts and led directly to the adoption of the Eleventh Amendment.

Martin v. Hunter's Lessee (1816).   See under JUDICIAL REVIEW.

Cohens v. Virginia (1821).   Though state courts may exercise final authority in cases that fall entirely within their jurisdiction, they are subject to the appellate jurisdiction of federal courts if their judgments involve the construction of federal laws or treaties or the Constitution. The Court also held that a federal court's review of a state court judgment against a defendant does not constitute a suit against a state prohibited by the Eleventh Amendment because the state itself initiated the lawsuit.

Ex parte McCardle (1869).   Congress may make exceptions to the Court's appellate jurisdiction even after hearings on a case have been concluded. McCardle had been tried for sedition by a military commission in Mississippi under authority provided by an act of Congress. He appealed to the Supreme Court. Some members of Congress feared that the Court would follow its precedent in *ex parte Milligan* (see under THE PRESIDENT AS COMMANDER-IN-CHIEF) and void the act. Congress thereupon repealed the legislation giving the Supreme Court jurisdiction to hear McCardle's case on appeal. Said Chief Justice Chase: "Without jurisdiction the court cannot proceed at all in any cause. Jurisdiction is power to declare the law, and when it ceases to exist, the only function remaining to the court is that of announcing the fact and dismissing the cause."

Nashville, Chattanooga, and St. Louis R. Co. v. Wallace (1933). The Court accepted jurisdiction to hear an appeal from a state court's "declaratory judgment," which was then a recent innovation. The Court said that the Constitution does not "crystallize into changeless form" the procedure of 1789 and, "so long as the case retains the essentials of an adversary proceeding, involving a real, not a hypothetical controversy, which is finally determined by the judgment below," it is a "controversy" as this word is used in conferring jurisdiction in Article III.

Pennhurst State School & Hospital v. Halderman (1984). Federal courts lack jurisdiction under the Eleventh Amendment to enjoin state and local officials because conditions in a state mental hospital violate state law.

DIVERSITY OF CITIZENSHIP

Swift v. Tyson (1842). In adjudicating cases (as authorized by Article III, section 2) between residents of different states that contain no federal question, federal courts must apply relevant state statutes but need not follow state court decisions based on the common law. Where no state statute exists, federal courts are free to develop their own common law. Overruled by *Erie Railroad Co. v. Tompkins* (see below).

Erie Railroad Co. v. Tompkins (1938). Tompkins, a resident of Pennsylvania, was injured while walking along the right-of-way of the Erie Railroad, a New York corporation. Under the common law of Pennsylvania, where the accident occurred, Tompkins was a trespasser and not entitled to damages. The lower federal court, however, applied its own rule and held the railroad negligent and liable for damages. The Supreme Court overruled *Swift* v. *Tyson* for several reasons: it allowed plaintiffs to select the court where the law was most favorable to them, state and federal courts located in the same state might decide the same case differently, and in matters not governed by the Constitution or acts of Congress, "the law to be applied in any case is the law of the State. And whether the law of the State shall be declared by the legislature in a statute or by its highest court in a decision is not a matter of federal concern. There is no federal general common law."

COMITY AND THE ABSTENTION DOCTRINE

***Railroad Commission* v. *Pullman Co.* (1941).** Formulated the "abstention doctrine" to minimize conflict between state and federal courts. Applications of this doctrine have produced a system of "comity" by which the federal courts substantially avoid intruding themselves into ongoing state judicial proceedings. Comity accomplishes this by requiring litigants to exhaust their state's remedies, administrative as well as judicial, before gaining access to the federal courts. The policy gives the state courts the first opportunity to determine the constitutionality of their own laws. If the state court acts compatibly with the supremacy clause of Article VI, section 2, and gives force and effect to the federal law, there may be no need for federal court intervention.

***Younger* v. *Harris* (1971).** The defendant sought to prevent being prosecuted for violation of a state law that he contended was unconstitutional. The Court said that a federal court may enjoin a state criminal prosecution only where there is "great and immediate" danger "of irreparable loss" of federal rights. No such danger existed here.

***Michigan* v. *Long* (1983).** The Court used this case, an otherwise run-of-the-mill vehicular search-and-seizure suit, to over-rule its traditional presumption regarding the "reviewability" of state court decisions. In cases where federal questions are bound up with issues of state law—which is true of most state criminal and civil rights litigation—the Supreme Court had declined review as long as the state court decision rested "on an adequate and independent state ground." In other words, if the state court would be able to adhere to its original decision notwithstanding a Supreme Court ruling on the federal aspects of the case, the Supreme Court would refuse to hear the matter.

Now, if it is unclear whether the state court based its decision on state or on federal law, the Supreme Court will presume that it rests on federal law and, as such, the case is reviewable. The effect of this holding, authored by Justice O'Connor, vastly broadens the Supreme Court's authority to review state court decisions. If it is adhered to and utilized regularly, the autonomy of the state courts will be undermined and seriously compromised.

THE FULL FAITH AND CREDIT CLAUSE

***International Shoe Co.* v. *Washington* (1945).** Formulated the "minimum contacts" test that prevents a state court from taking action against a nonresident defendant unless said defendant has had sufficient contacts with the state wherein the court is located so that the lawsuit "does not offend traditional notions of fair play and substantial justice," wrote Chief Justice Stone. As a result of this and subsequent decisions, the full faith and credit clause has the following scope and meaning: state court judgments in civil, not criminal, cases have as much force and effect in courts of other states as they do in the rendering state—provided that the court making the decision had jurisdiction, in a minimum contacts sense, over the litigants.

Most Supreme Court litigation involving full faith and credit traditionally involved divorce actions where the husband and wife resided in different states. Today most cases concern commercial transactions, insurance, and workers' compensation. Divorce litigation has faded because the states regularly recognize out-of-state decrees.

PRIVILEGES AND IMMUNITIES

Baldwin v. Montana Fish and Game Commission (1978). Reaffirmed a long line of precedents that limit the scope of "privileges and immunities of citizens in the several States" to those "fundamental rights" that bear "upon the vitality of the Nation as a single entity," according to the Court. Most assuredly, said the majority, "elk hunting by nonresidents in Montana is not one of them."

Hicklin v. Orbeck (1978). In order to reduce unemployment, Alaska required all gas and oil companies doing business within the state to hire only residents. The Court unanimously agreed that Alaska had failed to show that nonresidents caused Alaska's high unemployment rate.

Supreme Court of New Hampshire v. Piper (1985). No "substantial" reason, ruled the Court, supported New Hampshire's requirement that an attorney must live in the state in order to practice law in its courts.

INTERSTATE EXTRADITION

Kentucky v. Dennison (1861). Although Article IV speaks mandatorily, the Court refused Kentucky's demand that the governor of Ohio deliver up a fugitive from Kentucky justice. Said Chief Justice Taney: Given "the relations which the United States and the several States bear to each other ... the words 'it shall be the duty' were not ... compulsory, but [only] declaratory of ... moral duty." Hence, governors can use their discretion whether or not to honor extradition requests.

THE PLACE OF THE STATES IN THE NATION

Texas v. White (1869). No state may constitutionally secede from the Union. After the Civil War the governor of Texas sued to recover possession of United States bonds, acquired in 1850, that the secessionist legislature had sold to purchase supplies for the Confederate army. The Court held that Texas could recover the bonds. When entering the Union, a state becomes party to an indissoluble relationship. Hence, ordinances of secession and all other acts intended to give effect to it are absolutely void. "The Constitution, in all its provisions, looks to an indestructible Union composed of indestructible States."

Stearns v. Minnesota (1900). Congressional restrictions on Minnesota's taxation of public lands at the time it became a state could be enforced because the provision did not impair Minnesota's sovereignty or legal equality with the other states.

Coyle v. Smith (1911). Upheld the right of Oklahoma to change the location of its capital, contrary to a condition imposed by Congress when Oklahoma became a state. The location of its capital is a matter of state policy for state authorities to determine. And when admitted to the Union, Oklahoma became legally equal to every other state.

FEDERAL GUARANTEES TO THE STATES

Luther v. Borden (1849). This case arose in the aftermath of the Dorr Rebellion in 1841, during which two rival governments existed in Rhode Island. One was regularly elected by residents who met a long-standing property qualification for voting. The other (Dorr's) was based on an informal election under universal manhood suffrage. At the request of the older government, President Tyler ordered militia into the state, and Dorr's government collapsed. In construing Article IV, section 4 of the Constitution, the Court declined to say which government was "republican" in form or whether or not on this occasion the president had been justified in suppressing "domestic violence." The Court held instead that these are "political questions" to be resolved as they arise by Congress and/or the president.

Pacific States Telephone and Telegraph Co. v. Oregon (1912). Reiterated the holding of *Luther* v. *Borden* that the clause in Article

IV, section 4 guaranteeing a republican form of government is nonjusticiable. The company had requested the Court to invalidate a state tax enacted by popular initiative, contending that the initiative had made the government unrepresentative and therefore unrepublican.

CONTRACT CLAUSE

Fletcher v. *Peck* (1810).   The first decision to declare a state law unconstitutional. In 1796, the Georgia legislature attempted to repeal a huge grant of land corruptly made by the previous session of the legislature, the members of which had been bribed by speculators. The Court voided the recission. It considered the land grant to be a contract and, although legislative acts might be repealed, rights vested under prior acts could not be impaired.

Dartmouth College v. *Woodward* (1819).   The New Hampshire legislature could not constitutionally alter the charter of Dartmouth College without its consent. Corporate charters fall within the confines of the contract clause. The decision substantially immunized business and commercial interests from unilateral governmental action abrogating the terms and conditions of contracts and agreements freely made.

Charles River Bridge v. *Warren Bridge* (1837).   Sustained Massachusetts' charter to a competing company to build a bridge not far from an existing private toll bridge. The Court substantially modified the Dartmouth College decision by holding that the public interest and common-law rules of construction require that the provisions of public grants, charters, and franchises given to private corporations be strictly construed. The only powers bestowed are those specifically provided. They afford their holders no implied protection against legislative action that may lessen the charter's value.

Home Building and Loan Association v. *Blaisdell* (1934).   Upheld a state statute extending a mortgagor's right to redeem foreclosed property for two years beyond the time stipulated in the mortgage. The contract clause is not breached because the state may subject existing contracts to regulation in the public interest. Just as a state may come to the relief of its citizens in cases of natural disaster, so also may it act in an economic crisis to safeguard the economic structure on which the good of all depends.

THE BILL OF RIGHTS

Barron v. Baltimore (1833). Barron claimed that Baltimore's refusal to compensate him for a wharf rendered unusable by a city street-grading project violated the Fifth Amendment. The Court held the Bill of Rights applicable only to actions of the federal government, not to those of the states and their subdivisions. Chief Justice Marshall reasoned that the Constitution grants powers to government and that therefore the Bill of Rights could limit only the powers that had been granted. Furthermore, the Bill of Rights was added to the Constitution because the public feared oppression by the federal government, not the states. Effectively overruled by the Supreme Court's interpretation of the scope of the due process clause of the Fourteenth Amendment.

Gitlow v. New York (1925). Upheld a state law that made it a crime to advocate the duty, necessity, or propriety of overthrowing government by force or violence: ". . . the legislative body itself has previously determined the danger of substantive evil arising from utterances of a specified character," stated the majority of the Court. In the middle of the opinion, almost as an aside, appears the statement: "For present purposes we may and do assume that freedom of speech and of the press—which are protected by the First Amendment from abridgment by Congress—are among the fundamental personal rights and 'liberties' protected by the due process clause of the Fourteenth Amendment from impairment by the states." The Court offered no logical or historical justification for abandoning the rule of *Barron* v. *Baltimore* (see above). From this incidental beginning, almost all the provisions of the first eight amendments have by degrees been incorporated into the due process clause of the Fourteenth Amendment.

FREEDOM OF SPEECH

Schenck v. *United States* (1919). Sustained the conviction of a Socialist party official who had violated the Espionage Act of 1917 by urging young men who had been called for military service to assert their constitutional rights by opposing the draft. Justice Holmes, who wrote the opinion, suggested limitations for government encroachment on the First Amendment's guarantee of free speech: "The question in every case is whether the words used are used in such circumstances and are of such a nature as to create a clear and present danger that they will bring about the substantive evils that Congress has a right to prevent. . . . When a nation is at war many things that might be said in time of peace are such a hindrance to its effort that their utterance will not be endured."

Whitney v. *California* (1927). Sustained the conviction, under the California Criminal Syndicalism Act of 1919, of Anita Whitney, an organizer and executive committee member of the Communist Labor Party, which advocated sabotage, violence, and terror as means of effecting economic and political change. Though Miss Whitney testified that she did not believe in violence, the Court held that united and joint action by such a group involves greater danger to the public peace and security than the isolated utterances of individuals. Overruled by *Brandenburg* v. *Ohio* (see below).

Chaplinsky v. *New Hampshire* (1942). Freedom of speech does not include use of lewd, obscene, profane, or libelous expressions, or words such as "damned racketeer" or "God-damned Fascist." By their very utterance, such phrases inflict injury or tend to incite an immediate breach of the peace. "Fighting words" are "no essential part of any exposition of ideas" and are of such slight social value that the First Amendment does not protect them.

American Communications Association v. *Douds* (1950). Upheld a provision of the Taft-Hartley Labor Management Relations Act of 1947 that denied the facilities of the National Labor Relations Board to unions whose officials refused to take non-Communist loyalty oaths. The majority ruled that Congress did not violate the First Amendment when it used its commerce power to prevent political strikes fomented by agitators who had infiltrated labor unions.

Dennis v. **United States (1951).** Affirmed the conviction of eleven leaders of the American Communist Party under the Smith Act's prohibition of willfully advocating and teaching the overthrow of the government of the United States by force and violence. Citing Circuit Judge Learned Hand's interpretation of Justice Holmes' clear and present danger rule: "Whether the gravity of the 'evil,' discounted by its improbability, justifies such invasion of free speech as is necessary to avoid the danger," the Court decided that the danger here justified restraining freedom of speech. The government cannot wait "until the putsch is about to be executed, the plans have been laid and the signal is awaited."

Adler v. **Board of Education (1952).** Sustained a New York law that prohibited from holding any position in the public schools any person who advocated the overthrow of the government by force or violence. The statute authorized the Board of Regents to establish a list of organizations that advocated such action. Membership in an organization on that list constituted evidence to disqualify a person from public school employment. "School authorities have the right and duty to screen the officials, teachers, and employees as to their fitness in order to maintain the integrity of the schools," the Court stated. Overruled by *Keyishian* v. *Board of Regents* (see below).

Burstyn v. **Wilson (1952).** A state may not deny a license to show a motion picture on the ground that it is "sacrilegious." Motion pictures are "a significant medium for the communication of ideas" and thus are protected by the First Amendment.

Yates v. **United States (1957).** Mere advocacy of a revolutionary philosophy, such as that of Karl Marx, is not enough to convict a Communist Party member under the Smith Act. In order to convict, the prosecution must prove the accused guilty of advocating forcible overthrow of the government and of inciting others to take specific action toward this end.

Barenblatt v. United States (1959). See under Legislative Investigations.

Scales v. United States (1961). The First Amendment does not protect the speech or the association of an active member of a group, ostensibly a political party, if the group advocates forcible overthrow of the government. Neither does the due process clause of the Fifth Amendment protect an individual who was an active and knowing member of an organization that was conspiring to overthrow the government by force, even though the threat was not immediate.

Communist Party v. Subversive Activities Control Board (1961). The case arose out of an effort to compel the American Communist party to register under the terms of the Internal Security Act of 1950. The Court accepted the congressional conclusion that Communism is a movement dominated by the Soviet Union, a nation that is dangerous to the United States and its institutions. Hence, a requirement that the Communist party register with the Justice Department, list its members, and file financial statements does not violate freedom of expression or association. The Court, however, did not consider what, if anything, could be done to the Party if it refused to register.

Keyishian v. Board of Regents (1967). Overruled *Adler* v. *Board of Education* (see above) and voided New York's loyalty oath for teachers. A state may protect its educational system against subversion, but not by vague and uncertain methods that do not inform teachers of the sanctions involved in a complicated scheme of control that "cast a pall of orthodoxy over the classroom," according to the Court. The Court further stated that Communist party membership may not disqualify a public school teacher unless specific intent to further the unlawful aims of the party is shown.

Brandenburg v. Ohio (1969). Overruled *Whitney* v. *California* (see above) and held that the First Amendment does not permit a state to forbid advocacy of force or lawlessness as means to effect change "except where such advocacy is directed to inciting or producing imminent lawless action and is likely to incite or produce such action."

SYMBOLIC SPEECH

Stromberg v. California (1931). Invalidated California's "anti-red-flag" law in a case involving the display of a red flag at a children's camp. The peaceful display of a red flag as a "sign, symbol or emblem of opposition to organized government" is protected by the First Amendment. In Chief Justice Hughes' words: "The maintenance of the opportunity for free political discussion to the end that government may be responsive to the will of the people and that changes may be obtained by lawful means ... is a fundamental principle of our constitutional system."

Thornhill v. Alabama (1940). Declared unconstitutional a state law against "loitering or picketing," which, as interpreted by the state courts, prohibited a single picket from carrying a placard on the street in front of a factory. The Court, through Justice Murphy, held that peaceful picketing communicates the nature and causes of a labor dispute and thereby informs the public about a matter of public concern.

United States v. O'Brien (1968). Affirmed the conviction of a young man who, in order to influence others to adopt his antiwar beliefs, violated federal law by burning his draft card. An incidental limitation on First Amendment freedoms is justified if: it falls within the constitutional powers of government, it furthers an important or substantial governmental interest, the governmental interest is unrelated to the suppression of expression, and the incidental restriction on communication is no greater than necessary to further that interest.

Tinker v. Des Moines School District (1969). Voided a regulation banning the wearing of black arm bands to protest the Vietnam War. The Court majority found no relation between the regulation and student discipline. Students do not shed their freedom of expression "at the schoolhouse gate." Nor may they be "confined to the expression of those sentiments that are officially approved."

Cohen v. California (1971). A person may not be convicted of disturbing the peace because he wears a jacket in a courtroom emblazoned with the phrase "Fuck the Draft," the Court ruled. A state may not "forbid particular words without also running a substantial risk of suppressing ideas ..."

FREEDOM OF ASSEMBLY AND ASSOCIATION

De Jonge v. Oregon (1937).   Made the First Amendment right to freedom of assembly binding on the states. The Court reversed a state court's conviction of a speaker at a meeting called by the Communist party to protest police efforts to break up a strike. The right of peaceable assembly is essential in order "to maintain the opportunity for free political discussion to the end that Government may be responsive to the will of the people, and that changes, if desired, may be obtained by peaceful means."

Hague v. C.I.O. (1939).   Voided a Jersey City ordinance that required a permit from the director of public safety to conduct a public meeting. The Court held that people have a right to publicly assemble to communicate their views and to discuss public questions in an orderly and peaceful manner.

NAACP v. Alabama (1958).   Rejected Alabama's demand for the membership lists of the NAACP. The Court unanimously ruled that "inviolability of privacy in group association may in many circumstances be indispensable to preservation of freedom of association, particularly where a group espouses dissident beliefs."

Shelton v. Tucker (1960).   Ruled unconstitutional an Arkansas statute requiring public school teachers to list all organizations to which they belonged or contributed. The law, said the five-member majority, was overly broad. It "goes far beyond" what a "legitimate inquiry into the fitness and competency" of teachers warrants.

Edwards v. South Carolina (1963).   The state infringed petitioners' constitutionally protected rights of free speech, free assembly, and freedom to solicit redress of grievances when it broke up an orderly demonstration by two hundred students on the grounds of the state capitol and arrested their leaders.

Cox v. Louisiana (1965). Reversed a state court's conviction of a civil rights demonstrator for blocking a street. Since Louisiana had permitted labor unions and other organizations to block streets, it could not use a double standard for civil rights. The Court, however, warned that it would not sanction "demonstrations, however peaceful or commendable their motives, which conflict with properly drawn statutes and ordinances designed to promote law and order, protect the community against disorder, regulate traffic, safeguard legitimate interests in private and public property, or protect the administration of justice and other essential governmental functions."

Communist Party of Indiana v. Whitcomb (1974). Unanimously voided a state law barring from the ballot the candidates of any party whose officers had not taken an oath that the party did not advocate the overthrow of government by force or violence. The majority held that the law violated a First Amendment right to advance common ideas and cast an effective ballot. Four justices (the Nixon appointees) filed a concurring opinion arguing that inasmuch as the major parties' candidates had been listed on the ballot without their taking a loyalty oath, discrimination against the Communist party violated the equal protection clause of the Fourteenth Amendment.

FREEDOM OF THE PRESS

Near v. Minnesota (1931). Declared unconstitutional a state law directed at a weekly newspaper in Minneapolis that scurrilously attacked the integrity of law enforcement officials. The law prohibited the publication of scandalous, malicious, defamatory, or obscene matter and provided for enforcement by injunction against persons doing so. The Court held that the law prevented future publication and thus placed publishers under "an effective censorship," whereas freedom of the press means "principally, although not exclusively, immunity from previous restraint or censorship."

Grosjean v. American Press Co. (1936). Invalidated a Louisiana statute that imposed a heavy and discriminatory tax on the advertising revenue of newspapers in the larger cities of the state, most of which had opposed the Huey Long machine. The Court held that this action was "a deliberate and calculated device in the guise of a tax to limit the circulation of information to which the public is entitled."

New York Times v. Sullivan (1964). Libel laws cannot be used to "cast a pall of fear and timidity" over the press. Alabama courts had awarded heavy damages to Birmingham law enforcement officials who had sued the *New York Times* for inaccuracies in a paid political advertisement. The justices unanimously reversed this decision, holding that "debate on public issues should be uninhibited, robust and wide open," that injury to an official's reputation "affords no warrant for suppressing speech that would otherwise be free," and that a public official may not recover damages for libel unless he proves "actual malice," that is, that the statement was made "with knowledge that it was false or with reckless disregard of whether it was false or not."

Branzburg v. Hayes (1972). The majority rejected arguments that preserving the confidentiality of news sources is essential to the operation of a free press and held, 5 to 4, that a reporter must testify, and reveal the contents of his notebooks, to a grand jury. "We cannot seriously entertain the notion that the First Amendment protects a newman's agreement to conceal the criminal conduct of his source, or evidence thereof, on the theory that it is better to write about crime than to do something about it." Ergo: freedom *of* the press is not to be equated with immunity *for* the press.

Miami Herald Publishing Co. v. Tornillo (1974). Declared unconstitutional a Florida statute that gave a political candidate the right to reply to newspaper criticism of his character or official record. State-mandated publication intrudes on the right of editors to decide what their publications should contain.

Time, Inc. v. Firestone (1976). Sustained a libel judgment against *Time* magazine for publishing a sixty-seven-word report alleging that a socialite's husband was granted a divorce "on grounds of extreme cruelty and adultery" when, in fact, the decree specified no basis. Although the trial judge had observed that the proceedings "produced enough testimony of extramarital adventures on both sides to make Dr. Freud's hair curl," the Supreme Court ruled that Mrs. Firestone was a "private person," not a "public figure"; hence, the actual malice test of *New York Times* v. *Sullivan* (see above) does not apply. Instead, state courts may impose a standard of liability less protective of the media than where the plaintiff is a public official or a public figure.

FREEDOM OF THE PRESS VERSUS THE RIGHT TO A FAIR TRIAL

***Nebraska Press Association* v. *Stuart* (1976).**   Unanimously struck down a state court order restraining the media from publishing pretrial confessions made by a person accused of a ghastly mass murder. Chief Justice Burger declared that although "the guarantees of freedom of expression are not an absolute prohibition under all circumstances," barriers to prior restraint remain high. In a concurring opinion, Justices Brennan, Stewart, and Marshall wrote that the Constitution bars prior restraint as a means of ensuring a fair trial of an accused person.

***Zurcher* v. *The Stanford Daily* (1978).**   Sustained a search warrant of the offices of a student newspaper issued because the newspaper possessed photographs revealing the identity of demonstrators who had assaulted police officers. The Court held that the critical element in a reasonable search "is not that the property owner is suspected of a crime, but that there is reason . . . to believe that the 'things' to be searched for . . . are located on the property to which entrance is sought."

***Richmond Newspapers, Inc.,* v. *Virginia* (1980).**   The order of a trial judge closing a murder trial to the press and the public at the accused's request violated their First Amendment right to attend criminal trials. Absent an overriding interest, such trials must be open.

***Globe Newspaper Co.* v. *Superior Court* (1982).**   Declared unconstitutional a state law requiring the exclusion of press and public during the testimony of victims at criminal trials for sex offenses against minors. Though the protection of minors from further trauma or embarrassment is a compelling governmental interest, the First Amendment requires that the public's exclusion from criminal trials be established on a case-by-case, rather than a mandatory, basis.

OBSCENITY

Roth v. United States (1957). Affirmed a conviction for mailing obscene materials. The majority held obscenity to be beyond the pale of constitutional protection and defined it as follows: "Whether to the average person, applying contemporary community standards, the dominant theme of the material taken as a whole appeals to prurient interest."

Jacobellis v. Ohio (1964). Held a French film, *The Lovers*, not to be obscene because the contemporary community standards in the *Roth* definition of obscenity (see above) constitute a single national standard. "It is, after all, a national Constitution we are expounding." Overruled by *Miller* v. *California* (see below).

Memoirs v. Massachusetts (1966). Reversed a ruling that the book *Fanny Hill* was obscene because it was prurient and offensive, even though it had "some minimal literary value." To be obscene, a publication must meet three criteria: (1) an overall appeal to prurient interest, (2) patent offensiveness, and (3) "utterly without redeeming social importance."

Miller v. California (1973). By a 5 to 4 vote, the majority redefined obscenity: "A work may be subject to state legislation when that work, taken as a whole, appeals to the prurient interest in sex, portrays in a patently offensive way sexual conduct specifically defined in the applicable state law, and, taken as a whole, does not have serious literary, artistic, political, or scientific value." Nor did a jury need to apply national community standards. Overruling *Jacobellis* (see above), it could now use local ones.

Jenkins v. Georgia (1974). To be obscene, material must be hard-core pornography. Hence, a theater manager could not be convicted for showing a film (in this case, *Carnal Knowledge*) not X-rated, which received critical acclaim, and whose female lead was nominated for an Academy Award.

COMMERCIAL SPEECH

***Bigelow* v. *Virginia* (1975).** Paid commercial advertisements are not without First Amendment protection. A state may not constitutionally sanction a newspaper editor for publishing an out-of-state abortion clinic ad.

***Virginia State Pharmacy Board* v. *Virginia Citizens Consumer Council* (1976).** Individual consumers and society in general have a strong interest in the free flow of commercial information. Maintenance of professional standards does not justify a state's banning advertisements containing the price of prescription drugs.

***Bates* v. *State Bar of Arizona* (1977).** Invalidated a state disciplinary rule prohibiting lawyers from advertising. Such a restriction "serves to inhibit the free flow of commercial information and keep the public in ignorance," according to the Court. Routine legal services lend themselves to advertising and the legal profession is not demeaned thereby. But false, deceptive, or misleading legal advertising can be regulated.

***Bolger* v. *Youngs Drug Products Corp.* (1983).** The Court unanimously declared unconstitutional a federal statute that prohibited the mailing of unsolicited advertisements for contraceptives. In the opinion of the Court, Justice Marshall said: "The level of discourse reaching a mailbox simply cannot be limited to that which would be suitable for a sandbox."

FREE EXERCISE OF RELIGION

***Pierce* v. *Society of Sisters* (1925).** Invalidated an Oregon law that required parents to send their children to public schools until they had completed the eighth grade, thus preventing their attendance at accredited parochial and other private schools. The law unreasonably interfered with the liberty of parents to direct the upbringing and education of their children and deprives the parochial schools of their property and business without due process of law, the Court ruled.

Cantwell v. *Connecticut* (1940).   The First Amendment's guarantee of religious freedom, including an absolute freedom of belief and a qualified freedom of action, applies to the states. In reversing the convictions of three Jehovah's Witnesses, the Court declared that a government may not license religious solicitors or proselytizers because no official may constitutionally determine what is or what is not "religious."

Flag Salute Cases [*Minersville School District* v. *Gobitis* (1940) and *West Virginia State Board of Education* v. *Barnette* (1943)]. They involved the power to exclude children from the public schools because they refused, on religious grounds, to salute the American flag during school exercises. In the first case, the Court upheld the flag salute as a means of inculcating loyalty, holding that the requirement does not interfere with religious freedom. The second case, three years later, overruled the earlier decision. Any official effort to prescribe orthodoxy in politics or religion or to force persons to profess adherence to such orthodoxy violates the First Amendment.

Wisconsin v. *Yoder* (1972).   Unanimously voided the conviction of Amish parents who, on religious grounds, refused to send their children to high school.

Wooley v. *Maynard* (1977).   Declared unconstitutional a New Hampshire law that required most automobile license plates to display the state motto, "Live Free or Die." Jehovah's Witnesses attacked the law as repugnant to their moral, religious, and political beliefs. The Court ruled that an individual may not be required to participate in the dissemination of an ideological message by displaying it on his private property.

Thomas v. *Review Board of the Indiana Employment Security Division* (1981).   Denial of unemployment compensation to a Jehovah's Witness who voluntarily quit his job because a transfer would have required him to produce armaments, contrary to his religious beliefs, violated the free exercise of religion clause according to the Court.

ESTABLISHMENT OF RELIGION

Everson v. *Board of Education* (1947). Busing children to parochial schools so that parents can "get their children, regardless of their religion, safely and expeditiously to and from accredited schools," does not breach the wall of separation between church and state.

McCollum v. *Board of Education* (1948). School authorities of Champaign, Illinois, infringed the establishment of religion clause when they allowed representatives of Catholic, Jewish, and Protestant faiths to give religious instruction on school property during school hours, even though the school authorities did not pay for the religious instruction and enforced the attendance of only those children whose parents enrolled them in the program. Tax-supported schools may not disseminate religious doctrines and the compulsory-education law may not promote sectarian causes.

Zorach v. *Clauson* (1952). Upheld New York City's released-time religious education program that allowed students, at their parents' written request, to receive religious instruction during school hours on premises other than public school property. The Court construed the establishment clause less rigorously than in *McCollum* v. *Board of Education,* holding that it does not mandate absolute separation of church and state because, said the majority, "we are a religious people whose institutions presuppose a Supreme Being."

Engel v. *Vitale* (1962). Invalidated a twenty-two-word prayer composed by the State Board of Regents, New York's ultimate educational authority. The Court said of the prayer—which was to be recited at the start of each school day—"that it is no part of the business of government to compose official prayers for any group . . . to recite as part of a religious program carried on by government."

School District of Abington Township v. *Schempp* (1963).

Held that recitation of the Lord's Prayer or Bible reading during school exercises violates the First Amendment no less than reciting a composed school prayer. The Constitution requires a "wholesome neutrality" between church and state "that neither advances nor inhibits religion." This, however, does not prevent nonsectarian study of the Bible or religion in the public schools.

***Walz* v. *Tax Commission of the City of New York* (1970).** Upheld tax exemptions for properties used exclusively for religious purposes. These exemptions do not establish, support, or sponsor religion; they rather treat religious organizations the same as any other charitable, nonprofit entity. Moreover, restricting the fiscal relation between church and state tends to complement and reinforce the desired separation between them.

***Lemon* v. *Kurtzman* (1971).** Salary supplements to parochial schoolteachers and reimbursement of costs to teach secular subjects in private schools are unconstitutional. For such parochial programs to pass constitutional muster, three criteria must be met: they must serve "a secular legislative purpose," have a "principal or primary effect ... that neither advances nor inhibits religion," and "must not foster 'an excessive government entanglement with religion.' "

Chief Justice Burger, speaking for the Court, found numerous reasons why the programs could not be sustained: the religious purpose of the church-related elementary and secondary schools; the enhanced opportunities for religious indoctrination of children of impressionable age; the necessity for state surveillance of teachers to ensure observance of restrictions on course content; the necessity for state supervision, as well, of parochial school expenditures to determine which were secular and which were not; "the potential divisiveness" of "political division along religious lines," which would be "a threat to the normal political process"; and the "self-perpetuating and self-expanding propensities" of these innovative programs, given parochial schools' desperate need for money.

***Tilton* v. *Richardson* (1971).** Upheld 5 to 4 providing federal aid to construct academic buildings on church-related and other private colleges. College students are "less impressionable and less susceptible to religious indoctrination" than younger students; furthermore, a onetime, single-purpose construction grant causes few entanglements between church and state. The Court, however, did invalidate a provision that would have allowed religious use of the buildings after twenty years.

Mueller v. Allen (1983). By a 5 to 4 vote, the Court upheld tax deductions for public and private school tuition, fees, books, and transportation. No impermissible promotion of religion occurs because deductions may be taken by all parents regardless of whether their children attend public, parochial, or nonsectarian private schools.

Lynch v. Donnelly (1984). Inclusion of a nativity scene in a city Christmas display has a secular legislative purpose that does not impermissibly advance religion or excessively entangle the city with religion; namely, to celebrate a public holiday and the origins of that holiday.

Wallace v. Jaffree (1985). A moment of legislatively mandated silence in public schools "for meditation or voluntary prayer" runs afoul of the establishment clause. The record clearly indicates that the law's sole purpose is to return voluntary prayer to the public schools.

Grand Rapids School District v. Ball (1985). By a 5 to 4 vote, the Court voided a shared-time program in which classes in parochial schools were financed with tax dollars and taught by public school teachers. The program promoted religion in three ways: "The state-paid instructors, influenced by the pervasively sectarian nature of the religious schools in which they work, may subtly or overtly indoctrinate the students in particular religious tenets at public expense. The symbolic union of church and state inherent in the provision of secular, state-provided instruction in the religious school buildings threatens to convey a message of state support for religion to students and to the general public. Finally, the programs in effect subsidize the religious functions of the parochial schools by taking over a substantial portion of their responsibility for teaching secular subjects."

RIGHT TO KEEP AND BEAR ARMS

United States v. *Miller* (1939). Because a sawed-off shotgun is not the type of weapon a "well-regulated" militia uses, the Second Amendment does not apply to such guns and Miller's conviction for violating federal law was affirmed by the Court.

In decisions dating from the nineteenth century, the Supreme Court has consistently ruled that the Second Amendment does not bind the states. Hence, state and local governments are constitutionally free to enact gun control laws if they so desire.

UNREASONABLE SEARCHES AND SEIZURES

Mapp v. *Ohio* (1961). The exclusionary rule, which precludes the admission of evidence that the police unconstitutionally obtain, applies to state criminal prosecutions. In this case, allegedly obscene material seized without a search warrant, which could not have been admitted in a federal prosecution, also had to be excluded from a state prosecution.

Terry v. *Ohio* (1968). Upheld a "stop and frisk" law. When an experienced police officer observes unusual conduct that leads him to believe that a crime is about to be committed, he may "frisk" or gently pat down the outer clothing of the suspicious person. If weapons or other contraband is found, it is admissible as evidence.

United States v. *Matlock* (1974). Ruled admissible evidence seized in a warrantless search of a room occupied by a suspected bank robber and the woman with whom he lived. When the suspect was arrested in front of the house, he was not asked to consent to a search; his companion, however, admitted police officers to his room. The majority held that permission for a warrantless search may be obtained from "a third party who possessed common authority or other sufficient relationship to the premises."

Zurcher v. *The Stanford Daily* (1978). See under Freedom of the Press Versus the Right to a Fair Trial.

Mincey v. *Arizona* (1978). Reversed a decision of a state supreme court, which had approved a murder scene exception to the Fourth Amendment's search warrant requirement and the admissibility of the accused's subsequent confession. No emergency existed threatening the destruction or loss of evidence. A warrant could have been obtained quickly and easily. Mincey's statements while hospitalized in a barely conscious condition, isolated from his attorney and family, could not be considered voluntary.

United States v. Ross (1982).   Overruled the Court's 1981 decision limiting the scope of the automobile exception to the requirement of a search warrant. If police have probable cause to search a car, the search may extend to every part of the vehicle, including all packages and containers that may conceal the object of the search.

Illinois v. Gates (1983).   Overruled two Warren Court decisions for determining whether an informant's tip establishes probable cause for issuance of a search warrant. Six justices held that a "totality of the circumstances" approach is all that the Fourth Amendment requires.

United States v. Leon (1984).   Established a "good faith" exception to the exclusionary rule. Evidence secured under a defective search warrant (in this case, one issued without probable cause) may be used to prosecute the accused, provided the searchers did not know the warrant was defective.

WIRETAPPING

Olmstead v. United States (1928).   Federal agents did not violate the prohibition against unreasonable searches and seizures when, without actually entering a person's premises, they obtained evidence by tapping his telephone. (Six years later the Federal Communications Act prohibited anyone not authorized by the sender from wiretapping or publishing the substance of any intercepted communication.) Overruled by *Katz* v. *United States* (see below).

Katz v. United States (1967).   Overruled *Olmstead* v. *United States* (see above) and brought electronic surveillance within the purview of the Fourth Amendment. In *Katz,* a listening device was hidden in the top of a glass-enclosed public telephone booth often used by a suspected bookmaker. The police listened in only when the suspect used the booth. The Court held that a conversation is a "thing" that may be seized. Hence, the police invaded the suspect's privacy. All participating justices except Black agreed with Stewart's statement that "the Fourth Amendment protects people, not places. What a person knowingly exposes to the public, even in his own house or office, is not a subject of Fourth Amendment protection. . . . But what he seeks to preserve as private, even in an area accessible to the public, may be constitutionally protected."

United States v. United States District Court (1972). Declared unconstitutional a long-standing government practice of tapping, without prior judicial approval, the telephones of individuals who have no significant connection with a foreign government but who are suspected of domestic subversion. The Court held: "Fourth Amendment freedoms cannot properly be guaranteed if domestic surveillance may be conducted solely within the discretion of the executive branch. . . . Nor must the fear of unauthorized official eavesdropping deter vigorous citizen dissent and discussion of Government action in private conversation."

United States v. Kahn (1974). The Court, interpreting a recently enacted federal law, held that a district judge who finds probable cause that a home telephone is being used by the owner and "others as yet unknown" to conduct illegal gambling may properly issue an order to tap the telephone, and evidence so obtained may be used against them.

SELF-INCRIMINATION

Twining v. New Jersey (1908). Exemption from compulsory self-incrimination in a criminal proceeding is neither an immunity of national citizenship guaranteed against abridgment by the states under the Fourteenth Amendment nor required of the states by the standards of due process. Overruled by *Malloy* v. *Hogan* (see below).

Chambers v. Florida (1940). The police denied due process of law to four blacks when they obtained "sunrise confessions" after five days of interrogation in the absence of family, friends, or counsel "under circumstances calculated to break the strongest nerves and the stoutest resistance," stated the Court.

Adamson v. California (1947). A statute permitting judicial comment on the failure of a defendant to take the stand does not violate the self-incrimination clause. Reiterated earlier rulings that the due process clause does not require the states to adhere to the procedural guarantees of the Bill of Rights. Overruled by *Malloy* v. *Hogan*.

Ullman v. United States (1956). Upheld the constitutionality of legislation granting immunity from criminal prosecution to persons whose testimony in national security matters congressional committees demanded. A witness can be compelled to testify under such immunity even though loss of a job, denial of a passport, or public opprobrium may result. Protection against compulsory self-incrimination applies only to prosecution for crime.

Slochower v. Board of Higher Education (1956). Invalidated the discharge of a tenured professor in a municipal college who invoked the Fifth Amendment in a congressional investigation of Communist activity. Invocation of the self-incrimination clause provides only procedural protection; it does not imply guilt or professional incompetence.

Mallory v. United States (1957). Unanimously invalidated a confession because it had been obtained from a defendant who was detained by arresting officers for an unduly long time (about eighteen hours) before he was brought before a magistrate, in violation of the Federal Rules of Criminal Procedure.

Malloy v. Hogan (1964). Reversed a witness' contempt citation for refusing to answer questions on the ground that his answers might incriminate him. Overruled *Twining* v. *New Jersey* and *Adamson* v. *California* (see above) and made the self-incrimination clause binding on the states. The Court held it would be "incongruous to have different standards determine the validity of a claim of privilege" depending on "whether the claim was asserted in a state or a federal court."

Albertson v. Subversive Activities Control Board (1965). Voided provisions of the Internal Security Act requiring individual Communists to register, because admission of Communist affiliation would expose the registrant to criminal prosecution. Rendered inoperative provisions of other laws requiring the registration of the Communist party and Communist-front organizations.

Zicarelli v. New Jersey State Commission of Investigation (1972). Upheld a sentence for contempt of court of a witness who refused to testify when state laws provided that neither the testimony given nor leads therefrom could be used in any subsequent prosecution. The prohibition against compulsory self-incrimination had not been breached because the witness remained in the same position as if he had kept silent, according to the Court. Immunized individuals may only be prosecuted on evidence "derived from a legitimate source wholly independent of the compelled testimony."

MIRANDA WARNINGS

Miranda v. Arizona (1966). Extended the protection of the self-incrimination clause by requiring the police to clearly inform persons in custody prior to questioning them that they have the right to remain silent, that anything they do say may be used against them, that they have the right to consult an attorney, and that if they cannot afford an attorney, one will be provided them. Any questions answered by a person in custody who has not been given these warnings is not admissible as evidence against that person.

Harris v. New York (1971). Statements made by a suspect who had not been read the Miranda warnings, though inadmissible as direct evidence, may be used to impeach his courtroom testimony. The *Miranda* ruling, said the majority, "cannot be perverted into a license to use perjury"; the advantage of exposing false testimony outweighs the "speculative possibility that impermissible police conduct will be encouraged."

Doyle v. Ohio (1976). After receiving the *Miranda* warnings, defendants chose to remain silent. At trial, defendants claimed narcotics agents framed them. To impeach their testimony, the prosecutor cross-examined them about their failure to offer this alibi at the time of their arrest. The Court ruled that it is fundamentally unfair to allow an arrestee's silence to be used to impeach a courtroom explanation given *Miranda*'s assurance that silence carries no penalty.

Rhode Island v. Innis (1980). An offhand remark by a police officer does not constitute interrogation, even though the remark leads the suspect to incriminate himself. The Court stated that interrogation occurs only when "a person in custody is subjected to either express questioning or its functional equivalent." That is, "any words or actions on the part of the police that the police should know are reasonably likely to elicit an incriminating response from the suspect."

DOUBLE JEOPARDY

Palko v. Connecticut (1937). Sustained the right of a state to appeal a criminal case verdict. Palko, after having been convicted of second-degree murder, was retried, convicted of first-degree murder, and sentenced to death. Because double jeopardy is not "implicit in a scheme of ordered liberty," no constitutional violation occurred. In this case, all that the state sought was "a trial free from the corrosion of substantial legal error." Overruled by *Benton* v. *Maryland* (see below).

Louisiana ex rel. Francis v. Resweber (1947). A convicted murderer who had escaped death due to mechanical failure of the electric chair sought to prevent a second attempt at execution on the grounds of double jeopardy and cruel and unusual punishment. The Court held, 5 to 4, that the state's second effort to execute him does not violate the Constitution.

Bartkus v. Illinois (1959). The Court, 5 to 4, reiterated its position that the due process clause of the Fourteenth Amendment does not apply all the provisions of the Bill of Rights to the states. In this case, conviction for an offense (robbery of a federally insured loan association) in a state court, after the defendant had been acquitted of the same offense in a federal court, did not violate due process or raise any valid question of double jeopardy.

Benton v. Maryland (1969). Overruled *Palko* v. *Connecticut* (see above) and made binding on the states the Fifth Amendment's guarantee against double jeopardy. In a trial for burglary and larceny, the defendant was convicted of burglary but acquitted of larceny. On retrial (held because of errors in the burglary conviction), he was convicted of both larceny and burglary. The Court held that the larceny conviction subjected the defendant to jeopardy a second time.

Waller v. Florida (1970). An individual may not be prosecuted in a Florida state court for the same offense he was convicted of in a Florida municipal court. State and local courts are part of the same governmental entity, unlike state and federal courts. Compare *Bartkus* v. *Illinois* (see above).

Ashe v. Swenson (1970). A person acquitted of robbing one member of a group may not be retried on the same evidence for robbing a second member of the same group.

Crist v. Bretz (1978). The federal rule that jeopardy attaches when the jury is impaneled and sworn applies to the states as well.

TAKING OF PROPERTY BY GOVERNMENT

Berman v. Parker (1954). Congress did not violate the Fifth Amendment by authorizing the taking of private property to redevelop and make more attractive "blighted territory" in the District of Columbia. Once a public purpose for the taking is established, private enterprise may constitutionally be "one of the means chosen" to complete the project.

Penn Central Transportation Co. v. New York City (1978). "Diminution in property value, standing alone," cannot "establish a 'taking.' " The Court instead focused "on the character of the action and on the nature and extent of the interference." Here a landmark preservation law prohibiting the construction of an office tower above Grand Central Terminal does not take Penn Central's property.

Pruneyard Shopping Center v. Robins (1980). California's constitutional provision permitting individuals to distribute literature and solicit petition signatures in a privately owned shopping center does not take property.

Hawaii Housing Authority v. Midkiff (1984). A land reform act authorizing a state to take residential property from lessors and transfer it to lessees on payment of just compensation does not violate the Fifth Amendment's public use clause. A government properly exercises its power of eminent domain to lessen the concentration of land ownership in a few hands. Transferring the land so taken to private beneficiaries does not invalidate the taking. Government does not have to use the taken property itself to legitimate the taking.

THE RIGHT TO TRAVEL

Kent v. Dulles (1958). The secretary of state, in issuing passports under "such rules as the President shall designate," is limited to restrictions specifically authorized by Congress or established by usage. "The right to travel is part of the 'liberty' of which the citizen cannot be deprived without the due process of law of the Fifth Amendment."

Aptheker v. Secretary of State (1964). Declared unconstitutional those provisions of the Internal Security Act of 1950 that denied passports to persons belonging to organizations required by the act to register with the attorney general. The Court refused to uphold the restrictions because they are too broad; they do not consider whether a person's membership in such an organization is knowing or unknowing or whether his participation is active or inactive, and they do not consider the purpose for which one desires to travel.

Zemel v. Rusk (1965). Congress constitutionally granted the executive branch the authority to refuse to issue passports to American citizens traveling to Cuba. Such travel "might involve the Nation in dangerous international incidents."

TRIAL BY JURY

Strauder v. West Virginia (1880). Declared unconstitutional a statute requiring jury lists to be made up entirely of white male citizens. The statute violated the rights of blacks under the equal protection clause of the Fourteenth Amendment and deprived them of due process of law.

Hurtado v. California (1884). A state need not indict persons with a grand jury. "Information," certifying "probable guilt," suffices.

Maxwell v. Dow (1900). A state may use eight-person juries, instead of the twelve required in federal courts.

Patton v. United States (1930). Sustained a verdict reached by eleven jurors in a federal court. The twelfth had become ill after the trial had begun, and the defense and prosecution agreed to proceed without him. Inasmuch as a defendant in a federal court may waive a jury trial altogether, he may also consent to trial by eleven jurors. Absent such a waiver, federal courts must use twelve-member juries, a federal judge must superintend the trial, and the jury's verdict must be unanimous.

Norris v. Alabama (Second Scottsboro Case, 1935). Reversed the conviction of a black youth for rape because of a "long-continued, unvarying and wholesale exclusion of Negroes from jury service" in the county in which the trial occurred. Going behind the record in the case, the Court found that no black had ever been called for jury duty in the court and concluded that no black names had ever been placed on the lists of potential jurors, though many were qualified for jury service and some had served on federal court juries.

Duncan v. Louisiana (1968). Reversed a conviction in a non-jury trial for an offense for which the maximum sentence was two years in prison, even though Duncan received only sixty days. The

Court ruled that the right to trial by jury prevails in state criminal cases that, if tried in federal court, would require a jury.

United States v. Jackson (1968). Voided a provision of the Federal Kidnaping Act that authorized a jury to impose a death sentence if the kidnapper had harmed his victim. The Court said that the provision required a defendant to risk his life in order to obtain a jury trial.

Witherspoon v. Illinois (1968). Prohibited a death sentence when the jury that imposed or recommended it excluded prospective jurors who had expressed conscientious or religious scruples against capital punishment.

Taylor v. Louisiana (1975). Reversed a rape conviction because state law, for all practical purposes, excluded women from the pool from which jurors were chosen. The defendant was thus deprived of the right to be tried by an impartial jury drawn from a fair cross section of the community. Gender could no longer be a valid basis for determining eligibility for jury service. Overruled *Hoyt* v. *Florida* (1961), which had sustained exemption of women from jury duty on the ground that "woman is still regarded as the center of home and family life."

Ballew v. Georgia (1978). Conviction by a jury of less than six members deprives the accused of the right to trial by jury.

Burch v. Louisiana (1979). A state may not constitutionally convict a person of a nonpetty offense by a nonunanimous vote of a six-member jury.

Batson v. Kentucky (1986). See under RACE DISCRIMINATION.

Lockhart v. McCree (1986). Resolved a question that the Court had explicitly left open in *Witherspoon* v. *Illinois* (see above): whether persons opposed to capital punishment can be excluded from juries that determine the guilt as well as the sentence of persons accused of a capital offense. Such a practice, said the majority, does not violate the Sixth Amendment's requirements of an impartial jury or one representing a fair cross section of the community. Such excluded jurors are not a distinctive group and a state has the right to empanel a single jury that can impartially decide all the issues in a case.

RIGHT TO CONFRONT
AND CROSS-EXAMINE WITNESSES

Pointer v. *Texas* (1965). The Sixth Amendment's guarantee ˒ that an accused has the right to confront witnesses against him is binding on the states. Hence, the prosecution may not introduce a transcript of a witness' testimony at a pretrial hearing where the defendant was without an attorney and had no opportunity to cross-examine the witness.

Davis v. *Alaska* (1974). The credibility of a prosecution witness is impeachable by cross-examination even though the impeachment conflicts with a state's interest in preserving the confidentiality of juvenile delinquency proceedings.

Ohio v. *Roberts* (1980). Use of testimony given at a pretrial hearing when the witness could not be located to appear at trial does not violate the confrontation clause.

RIGHT TO COUNSEL

Powell v. *Alabama* (First Scottsboro Case, 1932). Reversed the conviction of a black youth for rape, on the ground that the trial judge had not effectively provided counsel for his defense. No attorney was appointed until the morning of the trial, which left no time to prepare a defense. "The right to be heard would be, in many cases, of little avail if it did not comprehend the right to be heard by counsel. . . . The failure of the trial court to make an effective appointment of counsel was a denial of due process."

Johnson v. *Zerbst* (1938). Reversed the conviction for forgery of a young marine who had informed the federal district judge that, though he had no attorney, he was ready to stand trial. Ignorant of the law, he failed to assert important rights while representing himself. An accused person may waive the right to counsel, but the waiver must be clearly and intelligently made. The trial judge has the "serious and weighty responsibility . . . of determining whether there is an intelligent and competent waiver by the accused."

Gideon v. Wainwright (1963). The right to counsel applies to state criminal prosecutions. Indigents accused of a felony have the right to be represented by appointed counsel.

Escobedo v. Illinois (1964). The police denied a murder suspect's repeated requests to consult his attorney. On the assumption that the same standard ought to apply in the stationhouse as in the courtroom (since what one says in the former place may be used in the latter, and statements resulting from lengthy inquisitions may jeopardize a person as much as courtroom admissions—arguably, even more. What happens in court occurs in full public view, unlike police interrogation), the majority held that "when the process shifts from investigatory to inquisitory—when its focus is on the accused and its purpose is to elicit a confession—our adversary system begins to operate, and, under the circumstances here, the accused must be permitted to consult with his lawyers." (Compare *Miranda* v. *Arizona* under MIRANDA WARNINGS.)

Argersinger v. Hamlin (1972). Extended the right to counsel to all cases in which a judge or magistrate wishes to preserve the option of imposing a jail sentence. No person may be sentenced to jail "without a knowing and intelligent waiver of his right" to counsel, stated the Court. If indigent, an accused must be provided with a lawyer's services.

Nix v. Whiteside (1986). An attorney's refusal to cooperate with the accused in presenting perjured testimony at trial does not deprive the defendant of effective representation by counsel. "Whatever the scope of a constitutional right to testify, it . . . does not extend to testifying falsely."

CRUEL AND UNUSUAL PUNISHMENT

Trop v. Dulles (1958). Declared unconstitutional a provision of the Nationality Act of 1940 that automatically revoked the citizenship of members of the armed forces who were convicted of wartime desertion.

Furman v. Georgia (1972). Held 5 to 4 that the death penalty was so infrequently and randomly imposed that it no longer credibly deterred crime. Hence, it constituted cruel and unusual punishment. Each justice delivered a separate opinion. Those in the majority said: The death penalty has in fact been imposed on a capriciously selected handful (Stewart). It is uniquely degrading and is tolerated only because of its disuse (Brennan). The threat of execution is too attenuated to service criminal justice (White). The death penalty falls disproportionately on the poor and minorities (Marshall). Capital punishment has no application to society at large, but only to some selected outcasts (Douglas). The minority justices disagreed about the value of the death penalty but all said that if it were abolished, abolition should result from popular action, not judicial decree.

Gregg v. *Georgia* (1976).   One of a group of cases in which the Court ruled the death penalty permissible if it were not imposed capriciously or arbitrarily, if the sentencing authority follows strict guidelines, and if it is not made mandatory for any particular crime.

Ingraham v. *Wright* (1977).   Disciplinary paddling of public school children is not cruel and unusual punishment, said a majority of five justices.

Coker v. *Georgia* (1977).   The death penalty may not be meted out for the nonfatal rape of an adult woman, according to seven of the nine justices.

Ford v. *Wainwright* (1986).   In its final death penalty decision, the Burger Court ruled 5 to 4 that the Constitution bars the execution of murderers who become insane while on death row. If such persons regain their sanity, however, they may be executed.

THIRTEENTH AMENDMENT: SERVITUDE

Pollock v. *Williams* (1944).   The Thirteenth Amendment prohibits all legislation that would compel a person to work in order to pay off a debt. A state may not "directly or indirectly command involuntary servitude even if it was voluntarily contracted for."

Jones v. *Alfred H. Meyer Co.* (1968).   Sustained an 1866 act of Congress that prohibited both public and private racial discrimination in the sale or rental of housing. The law had not previously been enforced, and similar civil rights legislation had been declared unconstitutional in 1883 (see the Civil Rights Cases under RACE DISCRIMINATION). Justice Stewart said for the Court that the Thirteenth Amendment was intended to remove "the badges and incidents of slavery" from the United States. "When racial discrimination herds men into ghettos and makes their ability to buy property turn on the color of their skins, then it too is a relic of slavery. The Thirteenth Amendment includes the right to buy whatever a white man can buy, the right to live wherever a white man can live."

FOURTEENTH AMENDMENT: CITIZENSHIP

Scott v. *Sandford* (1857).   A slave had resided with his master for several years in the free state of Illinois and at Fort Snelling, which was in a territory that had been made free by the Missouri Compromise. On returning to Missouri, Scott sued for his freedom. The Court held that neither Scott nor any other black—slave or free—could be a U.S. citizen. As a result, Scott could not sue under the diversity of citizenship clause of Article III of the Constitution. Furthermore, no constitutional provision protected blacks because "for more than a century before" the ratification of the Constitution, blacks had

> been regarded as beings of an inferior order; and altogether unfit to associate with the white race, either in social or political relations; and so far inferior, that they had no rights which the white man was bound to respect; and that the negro might justly and lawfully be reduced to slavery for his own benefit. He was bought and sold, and treated as an ordinary article of merchandise and traffic, whenever a profit could be made by it. This opinion was at that time fixed and universal in the civilized portion of the white race.

The majority accordingly declared the Missouri Compromise unconstitutional. Congress may not prevent citizens from transporting their slaves into a territory because slave ownership is a property right with which Congress may not interfere.

United States v. ***Wong Kim Ark* (1898).**   A child born in the United States and subject to its jurisdiction is an American citizen, even if his parents are aliens ineligible for naturalization. However, children born in the United States, but not subject to its jurisdiction, are not citizens. These include children of foreign diplomats, children born on foreign ships in American territorial waters, and Indians born on reservations. Congress later (1924) made all Indians American citizens.

***Perez* v. *Brownell* (1958).**   Upheld a provision of the Smith Act (1940) that a native-born American might forfeit citizenship by participating in an election in a foreign country. Under its power to legislate on foreign relations, Congress may prevent interference by Americans in the affairs of a foreign country. Overruled by *Afroyim* v. *Rusk* (see below).

***Schneider* v. *Rusk* (1964).**   Voided a section of the Immigration and Nationality Act of 1952 that deprived of citizenship a naturalized person who lived three consecutive years in his native land. Justice Douglas, for the Court, said that depriving naturalized citizens of a right that native-born citizens may exercise makes them second-class citizens.

***Afroyim* v. *Rusk* (1967).**   Overruled *Perez* v. *Brownell* (see above) and held that Afroyim, who had voted in an Israeli election, did not thereby lose his American citizenship. The Fourteenth Amendment's definition of citizenship binds Congress and prevents "forcible destruction" or deprivation of citizenship without an individual's consent.

THE FOURTEENTH AMENDMENT AS A LIMITATION ON STATE ECONOMIC REGULATION

***Munn* v. *Illinois* (1877).**   Sustained state regulation of grain elevators, with the Court declaring that the "public has a direct and positive interest" in private businesses "clothed with a public interest." Property put to such uses is subject to public control. As a consequence, the rates and services of public utilities could be regulated, notwithstanding judicial support for the principles of laissez-faire economics.

***Euclid* v. *Ambler Realty Co.* (1926).** Upheld a comprehensive zoning ordinance restricting and regulating the location of businesses, industries, and various types of dwellings. Despite the losses sustained by many property owners in the zoned areas, the Court held zoning to be a reasonable exercise of the state's police power—the power to regulate on behalf of public health, safety, welfare, morals, and/or convenience—and as such does not violate due process.

***Tyson* v. *Banton* (1927).** Invalidated a New York State law limiting the resale price of theater tickets, on the ground that ticket brokerage is not a business affected with a public interest. Hence, its regulation is not a legitimate exercise of the state's police power. Effectively overruled by *Gold* v. *DiCarlo* (1965).

***Nebbia* v. *New York* (1934).** Upheld governmental fixing of minimum and maximum prices of milk. The majority thus expanded the scope of regulation under the police power beyond the limited category of public utilities and virtually abandoned the concept that only "businesses affected with a public interest" could be regulated.

***West Coast Hotel Co.* v. *Parrish* (1937).** See under STATE LABOR REGULATION.

PRIVACY

***Griswold* v. *Connecticut* (1965).** Established a right to privacy independent of freedom of association, the Fourth Amendment, and the self-incrimination clause. At issue, according to Justice Stewart, was "an uncommonly silly law" that made the sale or use of contraceptives a criminal offense. The Court, citing a long list of precedents, said that "specific guarantees in the Bill of Rights have penumbras, formed by emanations from those guarantees that help give them life and substance." These penumbras "create zones of privacy." Douglas, speaking for the majority, rhetorically inquired: "Would we allow the police to search the sacred precincts of marital bedrooms for telltale signs of the use of contraceptives? The very idea is repulsive to the notions of privacy surrounding the marriage relationship." He concluded:

> We deal with a right of privacy older than the Bill of Rights—older than our political parties, older than our school system. Marriage is a coming together for better or for worse, hopefully enduring, and intimate to the degree of being sacred. It is an association that promotes a way of life, not causes; a harmony in living, not political faiths; a bilateral loyalty, not commercial or social projects. Yet it is an association for as noble a purpose as any involved in our prior decisions.

Eisenstadt v. Baird (1972). The Court refused to accept Massachusetts' argument against use of contraceptives by unmarried persons: "to protect purity, to preserve chastity ... and thus to engender in the State and nation a virile and virtuous race of men and women." The Court considered it "plainly unreasonable to assume that Massachusetts has prescribed pregnancy and the birth of an unwanted child as punishment for fornication." Chief Justice Burger dissented, believing it proper that only physicians dispense contraceptives.

Moose Lodge v. Irvis (1972). A provision in the Civil Rights Act of 1964 exempting from its coverage "a private club or other establishment not in fact open to the public" is constitutionally permissible. The right to privacy may take precedence over a racially open society.

Whalen v. Roe (1977). Sustained a state law that required the computerized listing of the names and addresses of every person obtaining a prescription for a dangerous drug, such as opium or amphetamines, against a charge that it invaded "zones of privacy." The law, said the majority, contains "careful safeguards against indiscriminate disclosure" and evidences "a proper concern with, and protection of, the individual's interest in privacy."

Bowers v. Hardwick (1986). The due process clause confers no right on consenting adult homosexuals to engage in oral or anal intercourse. In its opinion, the five-justice majority rejected the view "that any kind of private sexual conduct between consenting adults is constitutionally insulated from state proscription." Choices fundamental to heterosexual life—marriage, procreation, child rearing, and family relationships—were sharply distinguished from homosexual acts. The majority also emphasized the "ancient roots" of laws outlawing homosexual conduct and noted that "24 States and the District of Columbia continue to provide criminal penalties for sodomy performed in private and between consenting adults."

FAMILY RIGHTS

Meyer v. *Nebraska* (1923).   Voided a statute that prohibited teaching foreign languages in elementary schools and also forbade teaching any subject in a language other than English. The law unreasonably infringed on the liberty to teach and the liberty of parents to secure instruction for their children, both of which the due process clause of the Fourteenth Amendment protects.

Loving v. *Virginia* (1967).   The Court unanimously and emphatically voided laws prohibiting interracial marriage as a deprivation of liberty as well as a denial of equal protection.

Mathews v. *Lucas* (1976).   Provisions of the Social Security Act requiring illegitimate children to show dependency on their deceased father in order to qualify for survivor's benefits do not unconstitutionally discriminate against them. Although the act makes it more difficult for illegitimate than for legitimate children to qualify, the classification reasonably relates to a permissible governmental purpose: the likelihood of dependency only where documentary evidence—a legitimated birth, support order, or paternity decree—exists.

Lassiter v. *Department of Social Services* (1981).   Upheld a state's refusal to appoint an attorney to represent an indigent mother, who had been convicted of second-degree murder, in claiming custody of her child. By a 5 to 4 vote, the Court ruled that the state's invasion of Lassiter's rights was "not so serious or unreasonable as to compel us to hold that appointment of counsel to indigent parents is constitutionally mandated." A state, however, is free to do so if it wishes.

Santosky v. *Kramer* (1982). Due process requires "clear and convincing evidence" to terminate parental rights. The traditional standard, "preponderance of the evidence" in the issue, for example negligence, insufficiently protects parents' fundamental rights in the care, custody, and management of their children.

Palmore v. *Sidoti* (1984). A parent may not lose custody of a child because of remarriage to a person of a different race. Speaking for a unanimous Court, Chief Justice Burger said that "the reality of private biases and the possible injury they might inflict" are impermissible considerations "for removal of an infant child from ... its natural mother." Although "the Constitution cannot control such prejudices ... neither can it tolerate them."

ABORTION

Roe v. *Wade* (1973). The Court voided state laws that made abortions criminal offenses (except to preserve the woman's life or health). Such laws violate the due process clause of the Fourteenth Amendment, which protects the right to privacy. This includes a qualified right to terminate a pregnancy. The state, however, does have a legitimate interest in protecting the pregnant woman's health and the potentiality of human life, both of which interests grow and reach a "compelling point" at different stages of pregnancy. For the first three months, abortion procedures must be left to the judgment of the woman and her physician. For the second trimester, the state may regulate abortion procedures in order to protect the woman's life or health. During the final three months, the state may regulate abortions, or even proscribe them, except to preserve the life or health of the woman.

Planned Parenthood of Central Missouri v. *Danforth* (1976). Voided a state law requiring parental consent for an unmarried woman under eighteen and spousal consent for a married woman to obtain an abortion. The majority said that what the state cannot do itself, it cannot delegate to another and, although a husband may be deeply concerned about his wife's pregnancy, she bears the child and is the more directly and immediately affected.

Beal v. Doe (1977). One of three decisions that respectively hold that state refusal to use Medicaid funds for nontherapeutic abortions violates neither federal law nor the Constitution, and that public hospitals may constitutionally adopt a flat no-abortion policy. One result: A pregnant woman has a constitutional right to an abortion only if she can pay for it and can find a hospital or or clinic willing to perform the operation. Another result: Taxpayers are not compelled to pay for other people's abortions and hospitals can set their own medical policy.

Akron v. Akron Center for Reproductive Health (1983). Reaffirmed a woman's right to an abortion and barred a variety of curbs that increased their cost; for example, that all second trimester abortions be performed in a hospital, and that twenty-four hours elapse between consent and performance of an abortion. Such requirements are invalid unless justified "by a compelling state interest."

Thornburgh v. American College of Obstetricians (1986). The Burger Court's final abortion decision. Voided the requirements that physicians (1) provide patients with detailed information about the risks of an abortion and alternatives to abortion, (2) compile records of abortions available to the public, (3) use the method more likely to promote a live birth, and (4) have a second physician in attendance when an abortion is performed. "The states are not free," said the five-member majority, "under the guise of protecting maternal health or potential life, to intimidate women into continuing pregnancies."

HANDICAPPED PERSONS

Buck v. Bell (1927). Upheld compulsory sterilization of "mental defectives" under a statute that applied only to inmates of state mental hospitals and provided for notice, hearing, and judicial approval before sterilization. Justice Holmes, speaking for the Court, minced no words: "It is better for all the world, if instead of waiting to execute degenerate offspring for crime, or to let them starve for their imbecility, society can prevent those who are manifestly unfit from continuing their kind. The principle that sustains compulsory vaccination is broad enough to cover cutting the Fallopian tubes. . . . Three generations of imbeciles are enough."

O'Connor v. *Donaldson* (1975). Unanimously ruled that individuals cannot constitutionally be confined to mental institutions against their will and without treatment if they are dangerous to no one and capable of surviving in the outside world.

Youngberg v. *Romeo* (1982). Again unanimously, the Court held that involuntarily committed retarded persons have substantive due process liberty interests that require a state to provide minimally adequate training to ensure their safety and their freedom from undue restraint.

Cleburne v. *Cleburne Living Center* (1985). Although the Constitution does not provide the mentally retarded with special protection against governmental discrimination, a Texas city's denial of a zoning permit for a group home was so irrational as to be unconstitutional. The permit requirement "appears to us to rest on an irrational prejudice against the mentally retarded." The record reveals "no rational basis for believing that the [proposed] home would pose any special threat to the city's legitimate interests."

POVERTY LAW

Goldberg v. *Kelly* (1970). If state or federal law "entitles" a welfare recipient to certain benefits, then, the Court ruled, the due process clause requires government to adhere to certain "procedural safeguards" before the recipient is deprived of them: timely and adequate notice detailing the reasons for termination, an opportunity to present evidence orally and to confront and cross-examine adverse witnesses at a hearing prior to the termination of benefits, the right to retain an attorney, an impartial decision maker must conduct the hearing, and the decision maker's decision must rest solely on legal rules and the evidence presented at the hearing.

***Dandridge* v. *Williams* (1970).**   Reductions in welfare entitlements, as distinct from their termination, do not violate the Constitution if they are reasonably related to a legitimate governmental purpose or interest. Budgetary and fiscal constraints are such.

***Fuentes* v. *Shevin* (1972).**   Contracts between debtors and creditors and between buyers and sellers must comport with the requirements of due process—specifically, giving notice and conducting a hearing—in order for a seller to repossess property for nonpayment of debt.

***Mathews* v. *Eldridge* (1976).**   The due process clause does not always require an adversarial type of hearing prior to the termination of governmentally provided "entitlements," as specified in *Goldberg* v. *Kelly* (see above). Three factors determine what process is constitutionally required: (1) the importance of the entitlement to the individual recipient, (2) the importance of the government's interest, and (3) the "risk of an erroneous determination" of the private interest because of the procedures employed by the government. In this case, involving medical disability benefits, the decision turned on "routine, standard, and unbiased medical reports by physician specialists." Hence, an informal, nonadversarial hearing after termination suffices.

RACE DISCRIMINATION

Civil Rights Cases (1883).   The Court voided the Civil Rights Act of 1875, which forbade proprietors of public conveyances, hotels, restaurants, and places of amusement to refuse admission to a person because of race, color, or previous condition of servitude. The Court held that the Fourteenth Amendment prohibited only governmental discrimination, not that in which individuals and private organizations engage.

***Yick Wo* v. *Hopkins* (1886).**   Invalidated a San Francisco laundry licensing ordinance on the ground that it arbitrarily classified persons so as to discriminate against Chinese laundrymen.

Plessy v. Ferguson (1896).   Upheld a Louisiana law that required railroads to provide "separate but equal" accommodations for white and black passengers. The Court said that a law which recognizes a difference in color "has no tendency to destroy the legal equality of the two races." The Fourteenth Amendment was not intended to enforce "social, as distinguished from political, equality or a commingling of the races upon terms unsatisfactory to either." If the enforced segregation "stamps the colored race with the badge of inferiority," it is solely because "the colored race chooses to put that construction upon it." The elder Justice Harlan's dissent strongly presaged the Court's opinion in *Brown* v. *Board of Education* (see EQUAL PROTECTION IN EDUCATION), which overruled *Plessy.*

Buchanan v. Warley (1917).   Voided a city ordinance that sought to establish residential segregation by prohibiting a member of one race from occupying premises in districts where a majority of the dwellings were occupied by members of another race. The decision was circumvented by resort to restrictive covenants. These were later denied enforcement in *Shelley* v. *Kraemer* (see below).

Morgan v. Virginia (1946).   Invalidated a law requiring race separation on motor carriers on the ground that the law interfered with interstate commerce by disturbing the comfort of interstate passengers and limiting their freedom to select seats. The Court ruled that interstate buses require a "single, uniform rule to promote and protect national travel."

Shelley v. Kraemer (1948).   Denied judicial enforcement to restrictive racial covenants (long-term agreements between private parties limiting the right to own, lease, or occupy housing to members of only one race). The Court held that though such private voluntary agreements do not violate the equal protection clause of the Fourteenth Amendment, their enforcement by state courts does.

Washington v. Davis (1976).   Held that a racially neutral employment qualification cannot be considered discriminatory simply because a greater proportion of blacks fail to qualify than persons of other races or ethnic groups. A purpose or intention to discriminate, not merely a discriminatory effect, must be shown for a violation of the equal protection clause to occur.

Batson v. Kentucky (1986). By a 7 to 2 vote, the Burger Court, conservative on racial issues, overruled *Swain* v. *Alabama,* a conservative decision of the Warren Court, liberal on racial issues. A defendant may establish a prima facie case of purposeful discrimination, violative of the equal protection clause, when a prosecutor exercises his peremptory challenges to exclude blacks from a jury. (Such challenges permit an attorney to exclude a specified number of prospective jurors without any reason being given.)

EQUAL PROTECTION IN EDUCATION

Missouri ex rel. Gaines v. Canada (1938). Introduced a modification of the "separate but equal" doctrine regarding educational opportunities for blacks. Sustained a black's right to a professional education equally with whites by requiring that he be admitted to the all-white law school of a state university at least until a black law school was established. The Court explicitly rejected Missouri's offer to finance the student's legal education at an out-of-state institution as less than equal treatment.

McLaurin v. Oklahoma State Regents (1950). A black, admitted as a graduate student to the University of Oklahoma, was required by state law to occupy segregated seating in classrooms, the library, and the cafeteria. This policy denied him equal protection, ruled the Court, because it impairs "his ability to study, to engage in discussions and exchange views with other students, and, in general, to learn his profession."

Sweatt v. Painter (1950). The Court ordered a black admitted to the University of Texas Law School, from which he had been excluded because of his race, even though Texas had recently established a black law school. The justices observed that the separate facilities were not equal in faculty, course offerings, library, alumni achievements, or reputation.

Brown v. **Board of Education (1954, 1955).** Overruled *Plessy* v. *Ferguson*. The justices unanimously declared separate educational facilities to be "inherently unequal." They requested further argument concerning the means to achieve desegregation. In 1955, they ordered local authorities to "make a prompt and reasonable start" and instructed the federal district courts to "proceed with all deliberate speed" to end segregation in public schools.

Bolling v. **Sharpe (1954).** A companion case to *Brown* v. *Board of Education* that ordered desegregation of the public schools in the District of Columbia. There being no equal protection clause limiting the federal government, the justices based their decision on the due process clause of the Fifth Amendment.

Green v. **County School Board (1969).** Disallowed, as "intolerable," a school board plan to give parents "freedom of choice" to send their children either to a formerly all-white school or to a formerly all-black school, because the plan shifted responsibility for complying with *Brown* v. *Board of Education* from the school board to the parents. Declaring that the "time for mere deliberate speed has run out," the Court said that "the burden on a school board today is to come forward with a plan that promises realistically to work and that promises realistically to work *now*."

Swann v. **Charlotte-Mecklenburg County Board of Education (1971).** Addressed the means available for dismantling racially separate schools "in states having a long history of maintaining two sets of schools in a single school system ... to carry out a governmental policy to separate pupils in schools solely on the basis of race." Given that the objective remains the elimination of "all vestiges of state-imposed segregation" and that in pursuance thereof "a district court has broad power to fashion a remedy that will assure a unitary system," could courts order busing and the use of racial ratios to achieve this goal? The justices' unanimous response: Yes, indeed.

Noting that "bus transportation has been an integral part of the public education system for years, and was perhaps the single most important factor in the transition from the one-room schoolhouse to the consolidated school," the Court found "no basis for holding that the local school authorities may not be required to employ bus transportation as one tool of school desegregation. Desegregation plans cannot be limited to the walk-in school."

Racial quotas are also permissible. The Court was not saying that "any particular degree of racial balance or mixing" is required "as a matter of substantive constitutional right." But the presence of all-black schools creates a presumption of discrimination, and the use of racial ratios as "a starting point" in shaping a remedy therefore falls within courts' "discretionary powers." However, "the constitutional command to desegregate does not mean that every school in every community must always reflect the racial composition of the school system as a whole." This is a significant limitation: ratios and quotas are acceptable, but each and every school need not be balanced precisely. Indeed, the Court went further: "The existence of some small number of one-race, or virtually one-race, schools within a district is not in and of itself the mark of a system which still practices segregation by law." But if a district contemplates continuance of predominantly one-race schools, it bears "the burden of showing that such school assignments are genuinely nondiscriminatory."

***Milliken* v. *Bradley* (1974).** Cross-district busing between Detroit and fifty-three suburban school districts, said a five-member majority, may not be ordered to remedy purposeful segregation in one district unless it can be shown that the other districts had also acted unconstitutionally. The evidence showed that only Detroit had purposefully segregated its schools. A metropolitan remedy that encompassed both city and suburban school districts would also disrupt local control of school operations ("no single tradition in public education is more deeply rooted" than this) and would pose large-scale financial and administrative problems, to say nothing of the problems posed by the busing operation itself. In supporting the federal district court's metropolitan remedy, the dissenters emphasized that the state, not the local districts, is responsible for education, and asserted that a Detroit-only remedy could not effectively desegregate Detroit's schools inasmuch as they were already overwhelmingly black.

AFFIRMATIVE ACTION

Regents of the University of California v. Bakke (1978). A thirty-three-year old white student who had a medical aptitude test score slightly below that required for regular admission applied to a new University of California medical school at Davis. The school had reserved sixteen of 100 positions for blacks, Mexican-Americans, and other minorities. Persons occupying these positions had less distinguished academic records than Bakke, who was denied admission.

Six of the nine justices wrote opinions, with no single opinion garnering majority support. Four of the justices—Burger, Stewart, Rehnquist, and Stevens—considered the Davis quota system a violation of Title VI of the 1964 Civil Rights Act, which stipulates that "no person in the United States shall, on the ground of race, color, or national origin, be excluded from participation in, be denied benefits of, or be subjected to discrimination under any program or activity receiving Federal financial assistance." Citing the rule that the resolution of a constitutional issue should be avoided if a case can be fairly decided on a statutory ground, these four justices interpreted Title VI to mean that it should be color-blind in its application and concluded that the "ban on exclusion is crystal clear: Race cannot be the basis of excluding anyone from participation in a federally funded program."

At the other extreme were justices Brennan, Marshall, White, and Blackmun, who decided that the Davis program violated neither the Constitution nor Title VI. According to their view, preferential treatment is a permissible means "of remedying past societal discrimination," and Title VI was enacted "to induce voluntary compliance with the requirement of nondiscriminatory treatment." This being so, "It is inconceivable that Congress intended to encourage voluntary efforts to eliminate the evil of racial discrimination while at the same time forbidding the voluntary use of race-conscious remedies."

The opinion of Justice Powell, whose vote was decisive, refused to prohibit admissions officers "from any consideration of the race of any applicant." But because rights are personal, because " racial and ethnic distinctions of any sort are inherently suspect and thus call for the most exacting judicial scrutiny," and because the medical school had not been found guilty of discrimination, its quota system was unconstitutional.

***Fullilove* v. *Klutznick* (1980).** The enforcement clause of the Fourteenth Amendment, ruled the Court, permits Congress to require that 10 percent of federal funds for local public works projects be used to procure supplies or services from minority-owned businesses.

***Firefighters Local Union* v. *Stotts* (1984).** Title VII of the 1964 Civil Rights Act, which outlaws race or sex discrimination, also explicitly protects bona fide seniority systems that do not purposefully discriminate against minorities. Hence, an injunction prohibiting a "last hired, first fired" layoff to save the jobs of blacks cannot stand.

***Wygant* v. *Jackson Board of Education* (1986).** Declared unconstitutional a plan to lay off teachers that gave preference to racial minorities. However, public employers may establish affirmative action programs that serve an "important" or "compelling" governmental interest, according to the Court. One such interest is "remedying past or present racial discrimination." Furthermore, employers may begin affirmative action plans without a prior judicial finding of discrimination, and such plans need not be "victim specific." Instead, they may penalize individual whites who have not themselves discriminated. But such plans must be "narrowly tailored" to remedy past or present discrimination. Therefore, racial preferences in hiring or promotion are more acceptable than layoffs. "Though hiring goals may burden some innocent individuals," said the prevailing opinion, "they simply do not impose the same kind of injury that layoffs impose."

***Firefighters* v. *Cleveland* (1986).** Inasmuch as "Congress intended voluntary compliance to be the preferred means of achieving the objectives" of the employment discrimination provisions of the Civil Rights Act of 1964, a court may enter a consent decree in which employers, over the objections of white employees, agree to take preferential, affirmative action to promote or hire minorities, even though the decree benefits persons who were not actual victims of the city's race discrimination. Because of the voluntary character of consent decrees, judges may approve broader relief than in cases where the employer objects.

SEX DISCRIMINATION

Hoyt v. Florida (1961). The Warren Court's only sex discrimination case. A woman, convicted of murdering her husband with a baseball bat, argued that her all-male jury deprived her of the right to an impartial jury. Not so, said a unanimous Court:

> Despite the enlightened emancipation of women from the restrictions and protections of bygone years, and their entry into many parts of community life formerly considered to be reserved to men, woman is still regarded as the center of home and family life. We cannot say that it is constitutionally impermissible for a State, acting in pursuit of the general welfare, to conclude that a woman should be relieved from the civic duty of jury service unless she herself determines that such service is consistent with her own special responsibilities.

Overruled by *Taylor* v. *Louisiana*.

Cleveland Board of Education v. LaFleur (1974). Held mandatory pregnancy leaves for schoolteachers to violate due process of law. To assume that no teacher can perform her duties once she becomes four or five months pregnant and that she continues to be incapable until her child is at least three months old is "arbitrary" and bears "no rational relationship to the valid state interest of preserving continuity of instruction." So long as teachers are required to give "substantial advance notice" of their condition, "dates later in pregnancy" serve the state interest just as well, "while imposing a far lesser burden" on the exercise of the constitutionally protected "freedom of personal choice in matters of marriage and family life," especially since "the ability of any particular pregnant woman to continue at work past any fixed time in her pregnancy is very much an individual matter."

Craig v. *Boren* (1976).   Oklahoma prohibited the sale of "non-intoxicating" 3.2 percent beer to males under twenty one and to females under eighteen. Over the dissents of Burger and Rehnquist, the majority ruled that gender classifications withstand constitutional challenge only if they serve "important governmental objectives" and are "substantially related to achievement of those objectives." The "relationship between gender and traffic safety" is "far too tenuous" to satisfy this standard.

Califano v. *Goldfarb* (1977).   The Court declared a gender-based distinction in the distribution of Social Security benefits unconstitutional because it discriminated against widowers of female wage earners. Widows of male workers received survivor's benefits, but widowers did only if over half of their support came from their wives. It was discriminatory that widowers had to prove they were dependent, while widows were assumed to be so.

Rostker v. *Goldberg* (1979).   Upheld the constitutionality of the all-male draft and the exclusion of women from combat positions in the armed forces.

Mississippi University for Women v. *Hogan* (1982).   A state university may not constitutionally limit enrollment in its nursing program to women. Said Justice O'Connor's majority opinion, the school's policy is based on "the stereotyped view of nursing as an exclusively woman's job." The four dissenters maintained that the issue is the right of a state to honor women's "traditionally popular and respected choice" to attend a single-sex college.

Arizona Governing Committee v. *Norris* (1983).   Construed Title VII of the 1964 Civil Rights Act to forbid a state to establish a retirement plan that paid lower benefits to women than to men because of their longer life expectancy.

Hishon v. *King & Spalding* (1984).   The Civil Rights Act of 1964 (Title VII) forbids business partnerships—in this case a law firm—from discriminating against women employees (here by denying partnership to a female attorney).

ALIENS

Truax v. *Raich* (1915).   An Arizona statute requiring private employers to hire 80 percent of their workforce from among American citizens unconstitutionally infringes on alien's "right to work for a living in the common occupations of the community," ruled the court.

Graham v. *Richardson* (1971).   Because aliens are "a discrete and politically powerless minority," the Court held that state laws that discriminate against them are "inherently suspect and subject to close judicial scrutiny." Consequently, states may not condition eligibility for welfare benefits on U.S. citizenship.

Ambach v. *Norwick* (1979).   States may require governmental employees "who participate directly in the formulation, execution, or review of broad public policy" or who "perform functions that go to the heart of representative government" to be citizens, the Court stated. Thus, a city may exclude aliens from its police force. In this case, aliens may be made ineligible for certification as public schoolteachers. "Public education, like the police function, 'fulfills a most fundamental obligation of government to its constituency.' "

Plyler v. *Doe* (1982).   Texas law withholding funds from local school districts for the education of the children of illegal aliens violates the equal protection clause. Dividing 5 to 4, Justice Brennan's majority opinion asserted that though public education is not a fundamental right, denial of access thereto must serve a "substantial" state interest when it "imposes a lifetime hardship on a discrete class of children not accountable for their disabling status." Texas failed to show such an interest.

JUVENILE JUSTICE

Kent v. *United States* (1966).   Without granting a hearing, a juvenile court judge waived jurisdiction over a sixteen-year-old boy accused of housebreaking, robbery, and rape, thus permitting him to be indicted and tried in the regular adult courts, where the maximum sentences for these crimes are much greater. Speaking though Justice Fortas, the Court ruled that a valid waiver order requires a hearing on the matter, access by counsel to the social records and probation reports considered by the juvenile court, and a statement of the reasons for the waiver of jurisdiction. Absent these protections, "the child receives the worst of both worlds," getting neither "the protections accorded to adults nor the solicitous case and regenerative treatment postulated for children."

In re Gault (1967). A boy was committed to the state industrial school for having made an obscene telephone call, for which an adult would have received a $50 fine or been imprisoned for no more than two months. The majority declared that "the condition of being a boy does not justify a kangaroo court"; consequently, "neither the Fourteenth Amendment nor the Bill of Rights is for adults alone." The Court specifically required juvenile courts to give timely advance notice of charges; to guarantee the right to representation by counsel, either retained or appointed; to ensure confrontation and cross-examination of adverse witnesses; and to inform defendants of the privilege against self-incrimination and the right to remain silent.

Tinker v. *Des Moines School District* (1969). See under Symbolic Speech.

In re Winship (1970). In the first of its decisions concerning juveniles, the Burger Court prohibited juvenile courts from convicting minors unless the standard "beyond a reasonable doubt" is employed when the adolescent is charged with an offense that would be considered a crime if committed by an adult. The beyond a reasonable doubt standard, said the majority, "is a prime instrument for reducing the risk of convictions resting on factual error," for ensuring that "the moral force of the criminal law not be diluted by a standard of proof which leaves people in doubt whether innocent men are being condemned." The same considerations "which demand extreme caution in factfinding to protect the innocent adult apply as well to the innocent child."

McKeiver v. *Pennsylvania* (1971). The right to a jury trial in criminal prosecutions does not apply to juvenile delinquency proceedings. The Court stated: "If the jury trial were to be injected into the juvenile court system as a matter of right, it would bring with it ... the traditional delay, the formality, and the clamor of the adversary system and, possibly, the public trial."

***Goss* v. *Lopez* (1975).** Established public education as a property right of children. Accordingly, the Court ruled, students facing temporary suspension "must be given some kind of notice and afforded some kind of hearing." The notice can be oral or written. If the student denies the charges, "an explanation of the evidence the authorities have and an opportunity to present his side of the story" must be provided, and "as a general rule" the notice and hearing must precede "removal of the student from school."

***Parham* v. *J.R.* (1979).** Due process does not require a formal, adversary-type hearing before a parent or guardian may commit a minor to a state mental institution. The law recognizes "that natural bonds of affection lead parents to act in the best interests of their children."

***Santosky* v. *Kramer* (1982).** See under FAMILY RIGHTS.

***Schall* v. *Martin* (1984).** Statute authorizing pretrial detention for up to seventeen days of juveniles who present a serious risk of committing an offense does not violate due process. The statute serves legitimate state interests and satisfies procedural safeguards.

THE STATUS AND REGULATION OF INDIANS

The Cherokee Cases [*Cherokee Nation* v. *Georgia* (1831) and ***Worcester* v. *Georgia* (1832)**]. The Court held that Indian tribes are neither foreign nor subject nations but rather "domestic dependent nations" whose "relation to the United States resembles that of a ward to his guardian." The powers vested in an Indian tribe are the inherent powers of a limited sovereign that have never been extinguished. The federal government, but not the states, may deal with the Indians through its treaty-making power and the Indian commerce clause in Article I, section 9 of the Constitution.

***United States* v. *Winans* (1905).** Treaties between Indian tribes and the United States are not grants of rights to Indians.

They are grants of rights from them. The tribe reserves to itself all rights not granted to the United States.

***Williams* v. *Lee* (1959).**   Allowed the states a measure of authority in Indian affairs "in cases where essential tribal relations were not involved and where the rights of Indians would not be jeopardized"; for example, suits by Indians in state courts against non-Indians and state court jurisdiction over non-Indians who commit crimes against each other on a reservation.

***White Mountain Apache Tribe* v. *Bracker* (1980).**   Where a state asserts authority over the conduct of non-Indians on a reservation, federal courts must make a particularized inquiry into the nature of the state, federal, and tribal interests at stake. This inquiry is to determine whether, in the specific context, the exercise of state authority would violate federal law. The supremacy clause (Article VI) makes state law inapplicable when it conflicts with federal law or where federal regulation comprehensively occupies the field. Here Arizona's efforts to tax a logging company hired by a tribe to fell trees on its reservation conflicted with pervasive federal policies and regulations.

VOTING

***Ex parte Siebold* (1880).**   Let stand a federal conviction of a state-appointed election commissioner for violating both state and federal laws by stuffing a ballot box. Under Article I, section 4, Congress has plenary and paramount jurisdiction over the election of members of Congress and may supervise such elections "so as to give every citizen his free rights to vote without molestation or injury."

***Guinn* v. *United States* (1915).**   Voided Oklahoma's "grandfather clause," which required a literacy test for all voters in state and national elections except those who, under any form of government, were entitled to vote on January 1, 1866, or who then resided in some foreign nation, or were the lineal descendants of such persons. Though the law did not mention race, color, or previous servitude, the selection of a date prior to the adoption of the Fifteenth Amendment made it obvious that the intention was to disenfranchise black residents "in direct and positive disregard" of that amendment.

Harper v. Virginia State Board of Elections (1966). Delivered the coup de grace to the poll tax. Following passage of the Twenty-fourth Amendment, which banned the tax in federal, but not state, elections, only four Southern states retained it. Said the Court: A state violates the equal protection clause "whenever it makes the affluence of the voter or the payment of any fee an electoral standard." The amount of the Virginia fee: $1.50.

South Carolina v. Katzenbach (1966). With only a partial dissent by Justice Black, the Court upheld the constitutionality of the Voting Rights Act of 1965. As a result, Southern blacks, for the first time in history, were able to vote with relative ease.

The Voting Rights Act bans discriminatory practices, such as literacy and "understanding" tests in all fifty states, and also prohibits states from using any voting test if, in the 1964 Presidential election, fewer than 50 percent of their residents who were of age registered or voted. This provision applied to Alabama, Georgia, Louisiana, Mississippi, South Carolina, and Virginia, plus twenty-six counties in North Carolina, and a few counties in other states. Tests could be restored in these places only with the approval of the federal district court in the District of Columbia upon a showing that such tests had not produced racial discrimination in the preceding five years. Any new voting qualification has to receive the attorney general's approval. The act also authorizes the U.S. attorney general to appoint voting examiners to register applicants wanting to vote.

Oregon v. Mitchell (1970). Upheld the constitutionality of a 1970 amendment to the Voting Rights Act of 1965 that lowers the minimum voting age to eighteen in federal elections, but declared the provision unconstitutional for state and local elections. After the decision, Congress submitted and the state legislatures ratified the Twenty-sixth Amendment, which lowers the voting age to eighteen in all elections.

Dunn v. Blumstein (1972). Tennessee's requirements for voting in state elections (a year's residence in the state and ninety days in the county) violated the equal protection of the laws. "The State," said the Court, "must show a substantial and compelling reason" for such requirements because they impinge on the constitutionally protected right to travel from one state to another. And "any classification which serves to penalize the exercise of that right, unless shown to be necessary to promote a *compelling* state interest, is unconstitutional." No such interest had been shown. Durational requirements do not correlate with informed or intelligent voting. "Knowledge or competence has never been a criterion for participation in Tennessee's electoral process for long-time residents. Indeed, the State specifically provides" for absentee balloting by persons who "have only the slightest political interest, and from whose political debates they are likely to be cut off."

Rosario v. Rockefeller (1973).   Different concerns permit varying durations before voters may participate in primary elections. New York State required persons wishing to vote in a state primary to register eight to eleven months in advance. The law affected only new voters and those who wanted to change their registration from one party to another. This, said the majority, does not prohibit these voters from participating in primaries, but only sets time limits for the legitimate purpose of preventing a political raid by members of one party who switch to another. "Indeed, under the New York law, a person may, if he wishes, vote in a different party primary each year." By no means are voters locked "into an unwanted pre-existing party affiliation from one primary to the next." The four dissenters charged that the law unduly restricted party enrollment. Concern with raiding could be as effectively discouraged by a thirty- to sixty-day deadline. "Partisan political activities do not constantly engage the attention of large numbers of Americans, especially as party labels and loyalties tend to be less persuasive than issues and the qualities of individual candidates. The crossover in registration from one party to another is most often impelled by motives quite unrelated to a desire to raid or distort a party primary."

***Buckley* v. *Valeo* (1976).**   Invalidated portions of the Federal Election Campaign Acts that limit the amount of money a candidate or an independent group may spend in an election. Such laws, which ignore the high cost of media advertising in modern campaigning, excessively restrict "the number of issues discussed, the depth of their exploration, and the size of the audience reached." But the Court upheld limitations on contributions made directly to candidates and requirements reporting and disclosing money spent. Public financing of presidential elections was also sustained.

***Mobile* v. *Bolden* (1980).**   The Constitution does not guarantee the election of black candidates but only prohibits purposefully discriminatory voting standards, practices, or procedures. Mobile's at-large voting system is not such even though blacks, totaling more than 35 percent of the city's population, have never won election to the three-member city council.

Congress limited the applicability of the decision when, in 1982, it approved a twenty-five year extension of the Voting Rights Act. Voters no longer need to prove intentional discrimination to secure relief under the act, although they must still do so in lawsuits alleging violations of the Fourteenth and Fifteenth Amendments. Instead, minority voters may focus on the "totality of circumstances" surrounding a case, which show "an aggregate" of discriminatory results.

Qualifications, Powers, and Duties of Federal Officers

*   *   *   *

THE PRESIDENT (TERM, 4 YEARS)

Qualifications.   A natural-born citizen. Fourteen years a resident in the United States. At least 35 years of age.

Powers and Duties.   Execution of all laws. Makes treaties with advice and consent of Senate (two-thirds vote required). Appoints with advice and consent of Senate ambassadors to foreign countries, judges of the Supreme Court and of the inferior federal courts, and other officers of the national government. Recommends measures to Congress. Convenes extraordinary sessions of Congress. Has veto power over legislation unless repassed by a two-thirds majority. Commander in chief of the armed forces. Takes office January 20th. Limited to two elective terms and a maximum of ten years in office.

VICE PRESIDENT (TERM, 4 YEARS)

Qualifications.   Same as for President.

Powers and Duties.   Presiding officer of the Senate, with vote only in case of tie. Aids president, when requested, in foreign and domestic matters. Becomes acting president in cases of presidential disability. Becomes president if president dies, resigns, or is removed from office.

HOUSE OF REPRESENTATIVES (TERM, 2 YEARS)
435 MEMBERS

Qualifications.　At least 25 years of age. An American citizen seven years. Resident of state where elected.

Special Powers and Duties.*　Originates revenue bills. Originates and prefers impeachment charges. Elects president if electoral college fails to do so.

SENATE (TERM, 6 YEARS)
TWO FROM EACH STATE (100)
ONE THIRD OF THE MEMBERSHIP ELECTED
EVERY TWO YEARS

Qualifications.　At least 30 years of age. At least nine years a citizen. Must be a resident of the state from which he is elected.

Special Powers and Duties.*　Confirms presidential appointments. Approves or rejects treaties. Acts as court of impeachment. Elects vice president if electoral college fails to do so.

THE CABINET

An extraconstitutional body made up of the heads of the twelve executive departments and other high officers, such as the vice president and the director of the budget, who are invited by the president regularly to meet with him and give him advice.

Department	Date Created	Title of Head
State	July 27, 1789	Secretary of State
Treasury	Sept. 2, 1789	Secretary of the Treasury
Interior	March 3, 1849	Secretary of the Interior
Justice	June 22, 1870	Attorney General
Agriculture	February 9, 1889	Secretary of Agriculture
Commerce	March 4, 1913	Secretary of Commerce
Labor	March 4, 1913	Secretary of Labor

*These obviously do not include the general powers and duties common to both Houses of Congress; for example, the power to lay and collect taxes and to appropriate money.

Department	Date Created	Title of Head
Defense	Sept. 18, 1947	Secretary of Defense
Health, Education, and Welfare*	April 1, 1953	Secretary of Health, Education, and Welfare
Housing and Urban Development	Sept. 9, 1965	Secretary of Housing and Urban Development
Transportation	Oct. 15, 1966	Secretary of Transportation
Energy	Aug. 4, 1977	Secretary of Energy

Congress established a single Department of Commerce and Labor on February 14, 1903, but in 1913 two separate departments were created. The Department of the Army (formerly the War Department, established in 1789) and the Department of the Navy (established in 1798) were organized under the National Military Establishment in 1947 (name changed to Department of Defense in 1949). The secretaries of the separate armed services were deprived of Cabinet rank in 1947. The Post Office Department, created in 1829, was abolished by Act of Congress, August 12, 1970, and replaced by an independent publicly owned corporation. The postmaster general was removed from the Cabinet and from the line of succession to the presidency.

SUCCESSION TO THE PRESIDENCY

The vice president is the constitutional successor to the president. To provide for succession in case of the death, resignation, or disability of both the president and the vice president, Congress in 1792 put the president pro tempore of the Senate and the Speaker of the House second and third in line of succession. In 1886 this law was repealed and the succession devolved upon the heads of the executive departments approximately in the order of their creation. In 1947 Congress again changed the order of succession by placing the Speaker of the House and the president pro tem of the Senate immediately after the vice president and before the heads of departments. The present order of succession for

*In 1979 this department was divided by Congress into separate departments of Education and of Health and Human Services. The secretary of each is a cabinet member.

department heads is: secretaries of state, treasury, and defense, the attorney general, and the secretaries of interior, agriculture, commerce, labor, health and human services, housing and urban development, transportation, energy, and education. The adoption of the Twenty-fifth Amendment has greatly reduced the likelihood that any legislative or Cabinet member will succeed to the presidency.

IMPEACHMENT

Impeachment is an old English device for bringing formal charges against a public official for the purpose of removing him from office. It had been substantially supplanted by other means in England at the time the United States Constitution was written (Article I, sections 2 and 3, and Article II, section 4). Only one American president, Andrew Johnson, was impeached by the House of Representatives, but the Senate did not convict him. President Nixon resigned after the House Committee on the Judiciary voted three articles of impeachment against him. Since 1789, nine federal judges have been impeached, of whom four were convicted, but more than twice the number impeached have resigned prior to removal from office. The record suggests that the threat of impeachment has been more effective than impeachment itself. An officer, of course, may be indicted and tried by judicial process before or after impeachment.

Charts and Tables

*   ★   ★   ★

ENTRANCE OF STATES INTO THE UNION

Original thirteen states indicated by italics.

State	Settled	Area, Sq. Mi.	Entered Union
Alabama	1702	51,998	1819
Alaska	1783	586,400	1958
Arizona	1580	113,956	1912
Arkansas	1785	53,335	1836
California	1769	158,297	1850
Colorado	1858	103,948	1876
Connecticut	1635	4,965	1788
Delaware	1638	2,370	1787
Florida	1565	58,666	1845
Georgia	1733	59,265	1788
Hawaii	c500	6,449	1959
Idaho	1842	83,354	1890
Illinois	1720	56,043	1818
Indiana	1733	36,045	1816
Iowa	1788	55,586	1846
Kansas	1827	81,774	1861
Kentucky	1775	40,181	1792
Louisiana	1699	45,409	1812
Maine	1624	29,895	1820
Maryland	1634	9,941	1788
Massachusetts	1620	8,039	1788
Michigan	1668	57,480	1837
Minnesota	1805	80,858	1858
Mississippi	1699	46,362	1817
Missouri	1764	68,727	1821
Montana	1809	146,131	1889
Nebraska	1847	76,808	1867
Nevada	1850	110,690	1864

State	Settled	Area, Sq. Mi.	Entered Union
New Hampshire	1623	9,031	1788
New Jersey	1618	7,514	1787
New Mexico	1598	122,503	1912
New York	1614	47,654	1788
North Carolina	1650	48,740	1789
North Dakota	1780	70,183	1889
Ohio	1788	40,740	1803
Oklahoma	1889	69,414	1907
Oregon	1838	95,607	1859
Pennsylvania	1682	45,126	1787
Rhode Island	1636	1,067	1790
South Carolina	1670	30,495	1788
South Dakota	1794	76,868	1889
Tennessee	1757	41,687	1796
Texas	1686	262,398	1845
Utah	1847	82,184	1896
Vermont	1724	9,124	1791
Virginia	1607	40,262	1788
Washington	1845	66,836	1889
West Virginia	1727	24,022	1863
Wisconsin	1670	55,256	1848
Wyoming	1834	97,548	1890

TERRITORIES AND DEPENDENCIES

	Acquired	Area (Sq. Mi.)
American Samoa	1899—U.S. claims recognized by Germany and Great Britain in treaty	76
Canal Zone	1904—Leased in perpetuity from Panama*	553
Guam	1899—ceded to U.S. by Spain	206
Puerto Rico	1899—ceded to U.S. by Spain	3,435
Virgin Islands	1917—purchased from Denmark	133
Wake, Midway, and other Pacific Islands		42

*The 1978 Panama Canal Treaty provides for the turnover of the Canal to Panama, which will be completed on December 31, 1999.

PRESIDENTS OF THE UNITED STATES

No.	Name	Native State	Party	Term
1	GEORGE WASHINGTON (1732–1799)	Va.	Federalist	1789–1797
2	JOHN ADAMS (1735–1826)	Mass.	Federalist	1797–1801
3	THOMAS JEFFERSON (1743–1826)	Va.	Rep.-Dem.	1801–1809
4	JAMES MADISON (1751–1836)	Va.	Rep.-Dem.	1809–1817
5	JAMES MONROE (1758–1831)	Va.	Rep.-Dem.	1817–1825
6	JOHN QUINCY ADAMS (1767–1848)	Mass.	Rep.-Dem.	1825–1829
7	ANDREW JACKSON (1767–1845)	S.C.	Democrat	1829–1837
8	MARTIN VAN BUREN (1782–1862)	N.Y.	Democrat	1837–1841
9	WILLIAM HENRY HARRISON (1773–1841)	Va.	Whig	1841
10	JOHN TYLER (1790–1862)	Va.	Democrat	1841–1845
11	JAMES KNOX POLK (1795–1849)	N.C.	Democrat	1845–1849
12	ZACHARY TAYLOR (1784–1850)	Va.	Whig	1849–1850
13	MILLARD FILLMORE (1800–1874)	N.Y.	Whig	1850–1853
14	FRANKLIN PIERCE (1804–1869)	N.H.	Democrat	1853–1857
15	JAMES BUCHANAN (1791–1868)	Pa.	Democrat	1857–1861
16	ABRAHAM LINCOLN (1809–1865)	Ky.	Republican	1861–1865
17	ANDREW JOHNSON (1808–1875)	N.C.	Republican	1865–1869
18	ULYSSES S. GRANT (1822–1885)	Ohio	Republican	1869–1877
19	RUTHERFORD B. HAYES (1822–1893)	Ohio	Republican	1877–1881

Charts and Tables

No.	Name	Native State	Party	Term
20	JAMES A. GARFIELD (1831–1881)	Ohio	Republican	1881
21	CHESTER A. ARTHUR (1830–1886)	Vt.	Republican	1881–1885
22	GROVER CLEVELAND (1837–1908)	N.J.	Democrat	1885–1889
23	BENJAMIN HARRISON (1833–1901)	Ohio	Republican	1889–1893
24	GROVER CLEVELAND (1837–1908)	N.J.	Democrat	1893–1897
25	WILLIAM MCKINLEY (1843–1901)	Ohio	Republican	1897–1901
26	THEODORE ROOSEVELT (1858–1919)	N.Y.	Republican	1901–1909
27	WILLIAM H. TAFT (1857–1930)	Ohio	Republican	1909–1913
28	WOODROW WILSON (1856–1924)	Va.	Democrat	1913-1921
29	WARREN G. HARDING (1865–1923)	Ohio	Republican	1921–1923
30	CALVIN COOLIDGE (1872–1933)	Vt.	Republican	1923–1929
31	HERBERT C. HOOVER (1874–1964)	Iowa	Republican	1929–1933
32	FRANKLIN D. ROOSEVELT (1882–1945)	N.Y.	Democrat	1933–1945
33	HARRY S TRUMAN (1884–1972)	Mo.	Democrat	1945–1953
34	DWIGHT D. EISENHOWER (1890–1969)	Texas	Republican	1953–1961
35	JOHN F. KENNEDY (1917–1963)	Mass.	Democrat	1961–1963
36	LYNDON B. JOHNSON (1908–1973)	Texas	Democrat	1963–1969
37	RICHARD M. NIXON (1913–)	Calif.	Republican	1969–1974
38	GERALD R. FORD (1913–)	Nebr.	Republican	1974–1977

No.	Name	Native State	Party	Term
39	JIMMY CARTER			
	(1924–)	Ga.	Democrat	1977–1981
40	RONALD REAGAN			
	(1911–)	Ill.	Republican	1981–

JUDICIAL ORGANIZATION
OF THE UNITED STATES

Supreme Court.   Final jurisdiction over all cases arising in lower federal courts; over cases involving federal questions from highest state court having jurisdiction to hear the case.

Courts of Appeals.   11 in numbered districts into which the United States (except the District of Columbia) is divided, 1 in the District of Columbia.

>Final jurisdiction over cases arising in federal courts except those heard by the Supreme Court. In addition, the District of Columbia court of appeals has jurisdiction to review determinations of quasi-judicial federal commissions and cases arising in the District that in a state would be decided by the highest state court.

District Courts.   91 courts, at least 1 in every state; 1 in Puerto Rico; 1 in the District of Columbia.

>Original jurisdiction over cases arising under United States law. In addition, the Puerto Rico district court determines some matters arising under local law.

Special Courts.

Customs Court

Court of Military Appeals

Court of International Trade

Tax Court

Court of Appeals for the Federal Circuit

>Created in 1982 from the merger of the Court of Customs and Patent Appeals and the Court of Claims. Jurisdiction over such matters as appeals in suits for damages against the U.S.

and appeals from the Patent and Trademark Office, the Court of International Trade, the Merit Systems Protection Board, and the boards of contract appeals. It also has jurisdiction over patent appeals from the district courts.

District courts in Guam, the Virgin Islands, and Northern Mariana Islands

Jurisdiction over cases arising under the laws of the United States, as well as local laws.

Local courts in Puerto Rico

Jurisdiction over cases arising under local laws.

SUPREME COURT JUSTICES
SINCE 1789

The Supreme Court first consisted of a chief justice and five associate justices (*Judiciary Act of 1789*). The number of associate justices was reduced to four in 1801, increased to six in 1807, to eight in 1837, to nine in 1863, and reduced to six in 1866. The Act of 1869 provided for a chief justice and eight associate justices. This number has remained unchanged. Their term of office is for life unless a judge shall resign or be convicted on impeachment. It is interesting to note that in the entire history of the Supreme Court the only justice (Samuel Chase) impeached was acquitted.

Name	State	Term
(Boldface denotes chief justices)		
John Jay (1745–1829)	New York	1789–1795
John Rutledge (1739–1800)	South Carolina	1789–1791
William Cushing (1732–1810)	Massachusetts	1789–1810
James Wilson (1742–1798)	Pennsylvania	1789–1798
John Blair (1732–1800)	Virginia	1789–1796
Robert H. Harrison (1745–1790)	Maryland	1789–1790
James Iredell (1751–1799)	North Carolina	1790–1799
Thomas Johnson (1732–1819)	Maryland	1791–1793
William Paterson (1745–1806)	New Jersey	1793–1806
John Rutledge (1739–1800)	South Carolina	1795*

*Senate rejected his appointment Dec. 15, 1795.

The Constitution of the United States

Name	State	Term
Samuel Chase (1741–1811)	Maryland	1796–1811
Oliver Ellsworth (1745–1807)	Connecticut	1796–1799
Bushrod Washington (1762–1829)	Virginia	1798–1829
Alfred Moore (1755–1810)	North Carolina	1799–1804
John Marshall (1755–1835)	Virginia	1801–1835
William Johnson (1771–1834)	South Carolina	1804–1834
Brockholst Livingston (1757–1823)	New York	1806–1823
Thomas Todd (1765–1826)	Kentucky	1807–1826
Joseph Story (1779–1845)	Massachusetts	1811–1845
Gabriel Duval (1752–1844)	Maryland	1812–1835
Smith Thompson (1768–1843)	New York	1823–1843
Robert Trimble (1777–1828)	Kentucky	1826–1828
John McLean (1785–1861)	Ohio	1829–1861
Henry Baldwin (1780–1844)	Pennsylvania	1830–1844
James M. Wayne (1790–1867)	Georgia	1835–1867
Roger B. Taney (1777–1864)	Maryland	1836–1864
Philip P. Barbour (1783–1841)	Virginia	1836–1841
John Catron (1786–1865)	Tennessee	1837–1865
John McKinley (1780–1852)	Alabama	1837–1852
Peter V. Daniel (1784–1860)	Virginia	1841–1860
Samuel Nelson (1792–1873)	New York	1845–1872
Levi Woodbury (1789–1851)	New Hampshire	1845–1851
Robert C. Grier (1794–1870)	Pennsylvania	1846–1870
Benjamin R. Curtis (1809–1874)	Massachusetts	1851–1857
John A. Campbell (1811–1889)	Alabama	1853–1861
Nathan Clifford (1803–1881)	Maine	1858–1881
Noah H. Swayne (1804–1884)	Ohio	1862–1881
Samuel F. Miller (1816–1890)	Iowa	1862–1890
David Davis (1815–1886)	Illinois	1862–1877
Stephen J. Field (1816–1899)	California	1863–1897
Salmon P. Chase (1808–1873)	Ohio	1864–1873
William Strong (1808–1895)	Pennsylvania	1870–1880
Joseph P. Bradley (1813–1892)	New Jersey	1870–1892
Ward Hunt (1810–1886)	New York	1873–1882
Morrison R. Waite (1816–1888)	Ohio	1874–1888
John M. Harlan (1833–1911)	Kentucky	1877–1911
William B. Woods (1824–1887)	Georgia	1881–1887
Stanley Matthews (1824–1889)	Ohio	1881–1889
Horace Gray (1828–1902)	Massachusetts	1882–1902
Samuel Blatchford (1820–1893)	New York	1882–1893
Lucius Q.C. Lamar (1825–1893)	Mississippi	1888–1893

Name	State	Term
Melville W. Fuller (1833–1910)	Illinois	1888–1910
David J. Brewer (1837–1910)	Kansas	1890–1910
Henry B. Brown (1836–1913)	Michigan	1891–1906
George Shiras, Jr. (1832–1924)	Pennsylvania	1892–1903
Howell E. Jackson (1832–1895)	Tennessee	1893–1895
Edward D. White (1845–1921)	Louisiana	1894–1910
Rufus W. Peckham (1838–1909)	New York	1896–1909
Joseph McKenna (1843–1926)	California	1898–1925
Oliver W. Holmes (1841–1935)	Massachusetts	1902–1932
William R. Day (1849–1923)	Ohio	1093–1922
William H. Moody (1853–1917)	Massachusetts	1906–1910
Horace H. Lurton (1844–1914)	Tennessee	1910–1914
Charles E. Hughes (1862–1948)	New York	1910–1916
Willis Van Devanter (1859–1941)	Wyoming	1911–1937
Joseph R. Lamar (1857–1916)	Georgia	1911–1916
Edward D. White (1845–1921)	Louisiana	1910–1921
Mahlon Pitney (1858–1924)	New Jersey	1912–1922
James C. McReynolds (1862–1946)	Tennessee	1914–1941
Louis D. Brandeis (1856–1941)	Massachusetts	1916–1939
John H. Clarke (1857–1945)	Ohio	1916–1922
William H. Taft (1857–1930)	Connecticut	1921–1930
George Sutherland (1862–1942)	Utah	1922–1938
Pierce Butler (1866–1939)	Minnesota	1922–1939
Edward T. Sanford (1865–1930)	Tennessee	1923–1930
Harlan F. Stone (1872–1946)	New York	1925–1941
Charles E. Hughes (1862–1948)	New York	1930–1941
Owen J. Roberts (1875–1955)	Pennsylvania	1930–1945
Benjamin N. Cardozo (1870–1938)	New York	1932–1938
Hugo L. Black (1886–1971)	Alabama	1937–1971
Stanley F. Reed (1884–1980)	Kentucky	1938–1957
Felix Frankfurter (1882–1965)	Massachusetts	1939–1962
William O. Douglas (1898–1980)	Connecticut	1939–1975
Frank Murphy (1890–1949)	Michigan	1940–1949
Harlan F. Stone (1872–1946)	New York	1941–1946
James F. Byrnes (1879–1972)	South Carolina	1941–1942
Robert H. Jackson (1892–1954)	New York	1941–1954
Wiley B. Rutledge (1894–1949)	Iowa	1943–1949
Harold H. Burton (1888–1964)	Ohio	1945–1958
Fred M. Vinson (1890–1953)	Kentucky	1946–1953
Tom C. Clark (1899–1977)	Texas	1949–1967
Sherman Minton (1890–1965)	Indiana	1949–1956

Name	State	Term
Earl Warren (1891–1974)	California	1953–1969
John Marshall Harlan (1899–1971)	New York	1955–1971
William J. Brennan, Jr. (1906–	New Jersey	1956–
Charles E. Whittaker (1901–1973)	Missouri	1957–1962
Potter Stewart (1915–1985)	Ohio	1958–1981
Byron R. White (1917–	Colorado	1962–
Arthur J. Goldberg (1908–	Illinois	1962–1965
Abe Fortas (1910–1982)	Tennessee	1965–1969
Thurgood Marshall (1908–	New York	1967–
Warren E. Burger (1907–	Minnesota	1969–1986
Harry A. Blackmun (1908–	Minnesota	1970–
Lewis F. Powell, Jr. (1907–	Virginia	1972–
John P. Stevens (1920–	Illinois	1975–
Sandra Day O'Connor (1930–	Arizona	1981–
William H. Rehnquist (1924–	Arizona	1986–
Antonin Scalia (1936–	Illinois	1986–

Selected References

* * * *

Abraham, Henry J. *The Judiciary: The Supreme Court in the Governmental Process* (6th ed., 1983).

Baum, Lawrence. *The Supreme Court* (2nd ed., 1985).

Beard, Charles A. *An Economic Interpretation of the Constitution of the United States* (rev. ed., 1935).

Blasi, Vincent, ed. *The Burger Court* (1983).

Brant, Irving. *Impeachment: Trials and Errors* (1972).

Breckenridge, Adam C. *Congress against the Court* (1970).

Brown, Robert E. *Charles Beard and the Constitution* (1956).

Cahn, Edmond N., ed. *Supreme Court and Supreme Law* (1954).

Cannon, Mark W., and O'Brien, David M., eds. *Views from the Bench* (1985).

Cardozo, Benjamin N. *The Nature of the Judicial Process* (1921).

Carp, Robert A., and Stidham, Ronald. *The Federal Courts* (1985).

Carr, Robert K. *The Supreme Court and Judicial Review* (1942).

Clayton, James E. *The Making of Justice* (1964).

Corwin, Edward S. *The Doctrine of Judicial Review* (1914).

Crosskey, William W. *Politics and the Constitution in the History of the United States* (2 vols., 1953).

Curtis, Charles P. *Lions under the Throne: A Study of the Supreme Court* (1947).

Danelski, David J. *A Supreme Court Justice Is Appointed* (1964).

Ducat, Craig R., and Chase, Harold. *Constitutional Interpretation* (4th ed., 1987)

Dumbauld, Edward. *The Declaration of Independence and What It Means Today* (1950).

Farrand, Max. *Framing of the Constitution of the United States* (1913).

Fine, Sidney. *Laissez Faire and the General-Welfare State* (1956).

Frank, Jerome. *Law and the Modern Mind* (1930).

Frank, John P. *Marble Palace: The Supreme Court in American Life* (1958).

———. *Justice Daniel Dissenting* (1964).

Friedman, Lawrence M. *A History of American Law* (1973).

Garraty, John A., ed. *Quarrels That Have Shaped the Constitution* (rev. ed., 1987).

Goldman, Sheldon, and Jahnige, Thomas P. *The Federal Courts as a Political System* (3rd ed., 1985).

Grossman, Joel B., and Wells, Richard S., eds. *Constitutional Law and Judicial Policy Making* (3rd ed., 1987).

Hall, Kermit L., ed. *United States Constitutional and Legal History* (21 vols., 1986).

Halpern, Stephen C., and Lamb, Charles M., eds. *Supreme Court Activism and Restraint* (1982).

Hand, Learned. *The Bill of Rights* (1958).

Henkin, Louis. *Foreign Affairs and the Constitution* (1972).

James, Joseph B. *The Framing of the Fourteenth Amendment* (1956).

Jensen, Merrill. *The Articles of Confederation* (1948).

Kamisar, Yale. *Police Interrogation and Confessions* (1980).

Kelly, Alfred H., and Harbison, Winfred. *The American Constitution* (5th ed., 1976).

Konefsky, Samuel J. *The Legacy of Holmes and Brandeis* (1956).

Konvitz, Milton R. *The Bill of Rights Reader* (5th ed., 1973).

Kutler, Stanley I. *Judicial Power and Reconstruction Politics* (1968).

Levy, Leonard W. *The Supreme Court under Earl Warren* (1973).

Lewis, Anthony. *Gideon's Trumpet* (1964).

Malone, Dumas. *The Story of the Declaration of Independence* (Bicentennial ed., 1976).

Mason, Alpheus T. *The Supreme Court from Taft to Warren* (rev. ed., 1969).

McCloskey, Robert G. *The American Supreme Court* (1960).

McDonald, Forrest. *We the People: The Economic Origins of the Constitution* (1958).

McIlwain, Charles H. *Constitutionalism: Ancient and Modern* (rev. ed., 1947).

Murphy, Bruce Allen. *The Brandeis/Frankfurter Connection* (1982).

Murphy, Walter F. *Elements of Judicial Strategy* (1964).

———, Fleming, James E., and Harris, William F. III. *American Constitutional Interpretation* (1986).

Neely, Richard. *How Courts Govern America* (1981).

North, Arthur A. *The Supreme Court: Judicial Process and Judicial Politics* (1966).

O'Brien, David M. *Storm Center: The Supreme Court in American Politics* (1986).

Palmer, Benjamin W. *Marshall and Taney: Statesmen of the Law* (1966).

Paul, Arnold M. *Conservative Crisis and the Rule of Law* (1960).

Powell, Thomas Reed. *Vagaries and Varieties of Constitutional Interpretation* (1956).

Pritchett, C. Herman. *The Roosevelt Court* (1948).

———. *Civil Liberties and the Vinson Court* (1954).

———. *The American Constitution* (3rd ed., 1977).

Provine, D. Marie. *Case Selection in the United States Supreme Court* (1980).

Rodell, Fred. *Nine Men* (1955).

Rutland, Robert A. *The Birth of the Bill of Rights. 1776–1791* (1961).

Schlesinger, Arthur M., Jr. *The Imperial Presidency* (1973).

Schmidhauser, John R. *The Supreme Court: Its Politics, Personalities, and Procedures* (1960).

Schubert, Glendon A. *Quantitative Analysis of Judicial Behavior* (1959).

Schwartz, Bernard. *Super Chief: Earl Warren and His Supreme Court* (1983).

Selected References

Scigliano, Robert. *The Supreme Court and the Presidency* (1971).

Simon, James F. *In His Own Image: The Supreme Court in Richard Nixon's America* (1973).

Smith, Edward C., and Zurcher, Arnold J. *Dictionary of American Politics* (2nd ed., 1968).

Spaeth, Harold J. *An Introduction to Supreme Court Decision Making* (rev. ed., 1972).

————. *Supreme Court Policy Making: Explanation and Prediction* (1979).

Steamer, Robert. *The Supreme Court in Crisis* (1971).

Stern, Robert L., Gressman, Eugene, and Shapiro, Stephen. *Supreme Court Practice* (6th ed., 1986).

Swisher, Carl B. *The Supreme Court in Modern Role* (rev. ed., 1965).

Warren, Charles. *The Supreme Court in United States History* (1928).

Witt, Elder, ed. *The Supreme Court: Justice and the Law* (2nd ed., 1977).

————. *A Different Justice: Reagan and the Supreme Court* (1986).

Woodward, Bob, and Armstrong, Scott. *The Brethren* (1979).

Index Guide
to the Constitution

★   ★   ★   ★

PREAMBLE

ARTICLE I

Legislative Branch: organization, powers, and restraints.

ARTICLE II

Executive Branch: powers, restraints, duties, and election of the president.

ARTICLE III

Judicial Branch: powers, restraints. Definition of treason.

ARTICLE IV

Relation of states to each other and to the federal government. Guarantees to states. Government of territories.

ARTICLE V

Method of amending Constitution. Guarantee of equal representation of states in the United States Senate.

ARTICLE VI

Provision for national debts. Supremacy of the United States Constitution, federal laws and treaties. Pledge of national and state officials to uphold Constitution. No religious test required as qualification to public office.

ARTICLE VII

Method for ratification of the Constitution.

AMENDMENTS

The first ten amendments are called the Bill of Rights.

I   Freedom of religion, speech, the press, and assembly.
II   Right to keep and bear arms.
III   Limitation on quartering of soldiers in private houses.
IV   Limitation on searches and seizures.
V   Protection of personal and property rights.
VI   Right to speedy, public, and fair trial.
VII   Trial by jury in civil cases.
VIII   Excessive bail and cruel punishments prohibited.
IX   People possess other rights besides those enumerated.
X   Undelegated powers belong to the states or to the people.
XI   Exemption of states from suit by citizens of other states.
XII   Election of president (supersedes part of Article II, sec. 1).
XIII   Slavery prohibited.
XIV   Definition of citizenship. Guarantees of due process of law and equal protection of the laws against infringement by states. Constitutional adjustments to post–Civil War conditions.
XV   Right of adult male citizens to vote.
XVI   Congress empowered to impose an income tax.
XVII   Popular election of United States senators.

XVIII   Prohibition of intoxicating liquors for beverage purposes.

XIX   Right of women to vote.

XX   Change in congressional and presidential terms. Abolition of the "lame duck" session of Congress.

XXI   Repeal of the Eighteenth Amendment.

XXII   Limitation of president's terms of office.

XXIII   Presidential vote for District of Columbia.

XXIV   Poll tax prohibited in election of national officers.

XXV   Vice president to become acting president when president is unable to perform his duties.

XXVI   Suffrage extended to eighteen-year-olds in both state and national elections.

Index of Cases

★　　　★　　　★　　　★

Index of Cases

Index of Cases

Index of Cases

185

Index of Cases

27 million Americans can't read a bedtime story to a child.

It's because 27 million adults in this country simply can't read.

Functional illiteracy has reached one out of five Americans. It robs them of even the simplest of human pleasures, like reading a fairy tale to a child.

You can change all this by joining the fight against illiteracy.

Call the Coalition for Literacy at toll-free **1-800-228-8813** and volunteer.

**Volunteer
Against Illiteracy.
The only degree you need
is a degree of caring.**

Ad Council Coalition for Literacy

THIS AD PRODUCED BY MARTIN LITHOGRAPHERS
A MARTIN COMMUNICATIONS COMPANY